KINGDOM POWER

KOLAWOLE OBASEYE
COPYRIGHT © 2016

ISBN 978-978-952-156-2

Scripture quotations are taken from the king James version, the new King James version and the amplified bible

Published by
Kingsglory Publication
Kingsglory Avenue, Off Mukhtar Ramalan Yero Road, Gbagi Villa, Kaduna Nigeria

Contact : 08136891983 , 08098243341
email:kingsgloryassembly@gmail.com

TABLE OF CONTENT

INTRODUCTION

It is Heaven's expectation that the supernatural power of God be a natural way of life for all believers. Being a Christian means Christ lives in you and Christ is the power of God (1 Corinthians 1:24). Powerlessness is not an option or an excuse in Christianity. Once you become born again, you become a carrier of the power of God. Your encounter with Christ is an encounter with power:

> *...For the kingdom of God is within you...*
> *Luke 17:21.*

You can't claim to have the Kingdom and not carry power, which is the evidence of the Spirit of God that lives inside of you '...the kingdom of God is not in words but in POWER....' A Christian is not known by mere words but impact. He was configured to be the outlet of signs and wonders by the ability of the Spirit of God:

> *...and my speech...was not with enticing words of MAN'S WISDOM, but in demonstration of*
> *the Spirit and of power.*
> *1 Corinthians 2:4*

> *...ye shall receive Power, after that the Holy Ghost is come upon you...*
> *Acts 1:8*

The revelation of Jesus is about the manifestation of the wisdom and the power of God on earth. As a believer beholds him, God fills him more and more with His Spirit. The Spirit of God is the administrator of the power of God (1 Corinthians 12:11). God also unveils greater kingdom realities of the word (Jesus) through man. Everything we see in the book of Revelation: the seven Spirits of God, lightening, thundering, voices, etc are the realities in Heaven that should be expressed on earth. It will be the fulfillment of purpose when that happens but creation is still waiting and groaning for these manifestations. As a true son, do not rejoice over the 'little' manifestations you are seeing or have seen, instead, cry for all that is available in God for you

The Holy Ghost (the custodian of the power of God) is the ability of God that brings about that reality and He resides in you. As a result, take up the responsibility of making the earth look like heaven. You have no excuse for powerlessness. The kingdom of God is within you and it is evident only by the demonstration of power (Matthew 10:7, 8).

This book was birth from the place of revelation and encounters with God. As you read, expect an impartation of the power of God upon your life, which will enable you manifest the realities of heaven on earth. Remember, you owe the world an encounter with God!

Apostle Kolawole Obaseye
(Senior Pastor, Kingsglory int'l Ministries)
January, 2016.

CHAPTER 1
THE REALITY OF JESUS

For thine is the kingdom, the power and the glory." He is the king who oversees the kingdom: He is Christ which signifies power and He is the son which refers to glory.

Revelation 19:16.
"And He hath on His vesture and on His thigh a name written, KING OF KINGS, AND LORD OF LORDS."

I Corinthians 1:24.
"But unto them which are called both Jews and Greeks, Christ the POWER of God and the Wisdom of God"

Hebrews 1:2-3.
2. "Hath in these last days spoken unto us by His Son, whom He hath appointed Heir of all things, by whom also He made the worlds;

3. Who being the brightness of His GLORY, and the express image of His person, and upholding all things by the word of His power, when He had by Himself purged our sins, sat down on the right hand of the Majesty on high;"

Many try to be filled with God's power without going through Jesus and others try to enter the glory without the place of Jesus. you must understand that, you can't explore power without first having encountered Jesus. When your pursuit is all about the power and not the giver of the power, you may receive a little touch of it but be rest assured it won't last. The bible says except the branch abides in the vine, it won't bear fruit.

John 15:4-5.
4. "Abide in Me, and I in you. As the branch cannot bear fruit of itself, except it abide in the vine; no more can ye, except ye abide in Me.

5. I Am the vine, ye are the branches: He that abideth in Me, and I in him, the same bringeth forth much fruit: for without Me ye can do nothing."

Jesus said He is the vine and we are the branches. The branches are supposed to produce the fruits, but they cannot except they abide in the vine. Many refuse to abide and yet wonder why the don't see or manifest the glory. You must not lose your focus on Jesus at any point, if you want to carry power.

Your constant beholding of Jesus produces the glory and power you desire to have Jesus is more than just the cliché you use when closing a prayer. God is so particular about what you know about His Son Jesus, that was why he asked the disciples after three and a half years "who do you say I Am" (Matthew 16:13).

He wants to know how much revelation of his person has been communicated to you at each point of your lives.

You should take a break and ask yourself who is Jesus to me? You can be in the church or around religious activities, yet not know that Jesus Christ is not present. It is possible that you have lost touch of Jesus, even though, he is the essence of our Christianity. The focal point of everything you do. Once you lose essence of him, it is no more Christianity but mere religion. So when you notice powerlessness in your life, it tells you that your life is void of Jesus.

1 Corinthians 2:2.
"For I determined not to know anything among you, save Jesus Christ, and him crucified."

Jesus must be real to you. You must know him more passionately and more intimately. He must be more than what you talk about, more than whom you preach about or who you follow. You must have an intimate, personal contact with the person of Jesus.

Your relationship with Him should be intact and as a minister, you should go beyond the impression, the name, or fame and think about how much of the power and glory Jesus died to give you and how much of it is at work in you. You must be able to set up such momentum for the people. We must stir up a fire of the reality of the life of Jesus amongst the people of God that will outlive us. We have to go back to the root of our faith. As Paul said, I desire not to know anything but Jesus and him crucified.

Philippians 3:10.
"That I may know Him, and the power of His resurrection, and the fellowship of His sufferings, being made conformable unto His death."

By this kind of lifestyle and desire, we will raise a fire brand generation that is red-hot for Jesus, arrow-heads for the kingdom. So that wherever they go, they impact the next generation, a generation that will never allow revival to die in their time.

Where Do You Belong?

God wants to make himself real to those who desire to encounter Him. How can you have a master you don't know? How long will you keep describing the person in the light of what someone else told you. There were three kinds of people during Jesus' ministry on earth (John. 12:17-20).

1.   Those that bore records.
2.   Those that heard.
3.   Those that analyzed (they were sign boards), who said "the world has gone after him," but they exempted themselves.

Which of these categories do you fall into? Have you experienced Him personally? Or do you know Him by what people told you. Do you have an experience of who He is or are you trying to describe Him from what you read about Him?

The same came to Therefore to Philip, which was of Bethsaida of galilee and desired him, saying, sir we would see Jesus
John 12:21

Some people were there, among the sign longing crowd who made up their minds to see Jesus despite the miracles they saw they were not just going to have a festive season. They acknowledged that he is good; he does miracles, heals and lots more but they still pressed on to know Him, 'we want to experience Him, and see Him as He is'; beyond the flesh. Paul in scriptures says we know no man after the flesh neither do we know Christ after the flesh (2 Corinthians 5:16).

The proof of knowing or touching Jesus is that his personality, power and glory are seen in us. If you have met with Him you cannot remain the same: as we behold Him we are being changed into that same image.

2 Corinthians 3:18.
"And we all, with open face, beholding as in a glass the glory of the Lord, are changed into the same image from glory to glory, even as by the Spirit of the Lord."

Something definite will happen to you and people will know you have had an encounter with Jesus. It was said about the disciples; these are unlearned men (ignorant men) for they noticed they had been with Jesus (Acts 4:13).
There is always a testimony to prove your touch of Him. There is always a reality to show for it. For how long have you been with Him? Have you touched Him? Has your testimony affected people around you? Have you touched lives? Can men say, even if you don't testify, that something has happened to you? When you touch him, it will spark up a revival within you (John 4:28 & 29). He's not a charm but a life, not something religious or a feeling but a reality. When He speaks to you, it is His reality He releases.

John 6:63.
"It is the Spirit who gives life; the flesh is no help at all. The words that I have spoken to you are spirit and life."

His words make tremendous effect in your life. When He touches you, He puts a hunger within you that makes you unsatisfied and forever long for Him.
Little wonder why we can't convince the world about Christ, because you can't convince others about what you have not experienced. When you encounter Jesus, your heart burns for more of him (Luke. 24:13-32). A transformation takes place in your spirit and becomes visible in you for others to see.
We were configured to live in God's presence before sin came into place. So our hearts must always have a touch of Him, lest we start getting dried up in our Christian walk. Outside His presence, you are not protected; you are not under His blessing. so desire to know Him experientially.

Deep Calleth Unto Deep

The bible says a man through desire separates himself and intermingles with all kinds of wisdom (Proverbs 18:1). Every desire to know Him would compel a separation. Man will always live with emptiness till he experiences God, because there's a desire for God that is locked up in the heart of every man. It is eternity locked up within our hearts (Ecclesiastes 3:11). It is a reality that if you don't touch, you cannot be satisfied.

Psalms 42:7.
"Deep calls to deep at the roar of your waterfalls; all your breakers and your waves have gone over me."

The Deep is that eternity in man. The deep(eternity) in you calls for the deep(eternity) in God. Scripture says the Holy Ghost searches even the deep things of God (1 Corinthians 2:10). It is the Holy Ghost that can satisfy that longing. He alone understands the eternity of God.

It is a fountain that needs to be broken, that's why man looks for other things to satisfy him, but after sometime, he loses pleasure in such.

Except the Holy Ghost touches the eternity in you, no amount of message will satisfy you. The bible says, now the Lord is that Spirit and where the Spirit of the lord is, there is liberty. The liberty is to live as Jesus, to live in the reality of what He has prepared for you. Liberty of sonship and to become who you were created to be. Eternity must find eternity. Every pleasure you get from anything under the sun outside God is vanity, because after a while, it loses value. There is a satisfaction that spurs wisdom, understanding and knowledge, this happens when your deep meets his deep.

Revelation 2:4.
"Nevertheless I have somewhat against thee, because thou hast left thy first love."

The first love experience is what anchors the faith of every true believer. Paul said I count all things as dung for the excellence of the knowledge of the glory of God (Philippians 3:8). When you touch Him, you lose taste for everything else. When you know Him, it will be evident! Paul said; "that I may know Him and the power of His resurrection and the fellowship of His suffering". It takes someone who has touched Him, to desire the fellowship of His suffering.

Have you ever loved someone to a point that you want to feel the pains he feels? The bible says no greater love has anyone shown than that which Christ showed; He laid down His own life for us (John 15:13). If you have not experienced it, your walk with God will be shallow.

We have made the worship of God emotional and instrument oriented; so that when we do not feel like it or lack the needed musical equipments, our worship dies. We must know Him intimately beyond all these things.

Jesus is the syllable of our Christianity and our existence. When you know Him, all you look forward to is bridging the gap between you and Him. The reality of Jesus makes you hungry for Him, until it is no longer you but Him that lives in you.

Galatians 2:20.
"I have been crucified with Christ. It is no longer I who live, but Christ who lives in me. And the life I now live in the flesh I live by faith in the Son of God, who loved me and gave Himself for me."

Paul and all the disciples had an experience with Jesus. When we read of them, it should spur a hunger to want to have such an experience. You can't represent what you have not seen, heard or handled.

Jesus our Perfect Model

1 John 4:17.
"By this is love perfected with us, so that we may have confidence for the Day of Judgment, because as He is so also are we in this world."

Once you believe a lie, you empower the devil.

When you don't have a perfect picture of Jesus, you will struggle with demons. Scripture says "casting down every vain imagination that exalts itself above the knowledge of Christ." The vain imagination is the enemy's stronghold. A stronghold is a pattern of thought that is not in alignment with scriptures. It determines what controls your way of life. We must look like Jesus because he is the perfect model that we must follow and whatever is not found in him should not be seen in us.

We are called to look like Him, for that reason, we must press in and contend until we become like Him, so that we can help others become like Him.

Until you are desperate, you cannot pull what is in eternity into time. Our generation must rise up and produce reality. We must live for Him, so that ministry becomes a by-product of our intimacy and relationship with Christ. It is the outflow of an intercourse. We are not to do ministry but stay with Him and then the ministry will manifest itself.

Jesus: the Wisdom and Power of God

The supernatural should be a norm in the church. Something in your heart tells you, you are born for something greater than this. You are looking for something more than normal.

Man was configured and wired up to live in the supernatural that is why he can never be satisfied in whatever he does outside the supernatural. When God created man he gave him the mandate "rule thou in the midst of thy enemy," that is why man is never satisfied with his level of power because he was meant to rule both heaven and earth through a dimension of the power of God. He will always seek for power even when he does not need it; he just wants to be powerful because it is part of his makeup, to carry power.

When you are powerless, you remain in a state of dissatisfaction. It is amazing that the church makes excuses for her powerlessness; we are not supposed to give a reason for our inability to solve the world's problems.

We are not to give reasons for our failures, neither are we supposed to give reasons why people are not healed.

Matthew 10:8
"Heal the sick, cleanse the lepers, and raise the dead, cast out devils: freely ye have received, freely give."

The bible says we should raise the dead: what faith does the dead need to be raised? my faith. Let our faith work for them (what faith does a mad man need to be healed?). These things must provoke us to understand God's wisdom of operation.

Mark 6:2
"......what wisdom is this which is given unto him, that even such mighty works are wrought by his hands"

There are basically three types of wisdom:

Proverbs 18:1.
"Through desire, a man, having separated himself, seeketh and intermeddleth with ALL kinds of wisdom."

1. The wisdom of man.
2. The wisdom of this world.
3. The wisdom of God.

The wisdom of man is a kind of wisdom where a man uses all his smartness and expertise yet, cannot produce the required result (The bible says the world through this wisdom does not know God).

Our secular Education is from man not from God and through this wisdom, man has not found God or produce God kind of result.

1 Corinthians 2:4.
4. "And my speech and my preaching was not with enticing words of MAN'S WISDOM, but in demonstration of the Spirit and of power:"

Then he moves on to the next, which is the wisdom of this world, the prince of the air. It is used to represent all kinds of diabolical and satanic practices existing in the world.

1 Corinthians 3:19.
19. "For THE WISDOM OF THIS WORLD is foolishness with God. For it is written, He taketh the wise in their own craftiness."

There is the third kind of wisdom which is the one that comes from God.

Ephesians 3:10.
10. "To the intent that now unto the principalities and powers in heavenly places might be known by the church the manifold WISDOM OF GOD."

Wisdom is the Reality of Jesus

Wisdom is not manifested in words. When you have wisdom, there should be proofs. Wisdom is not saying things but manifesting them (1Corinthians 2:1-5). Jesus is the wisdom and the power of God, so the wisdom of God must have evidence of power.

Deuteronomy 34:10-11.
" and there arose not a prophet since in Israel like unto Moses, whom the lord knew face to face, in all the signs and wonder, which the lord sent him to do in the land of Egypt to pharaoh, and all his servant, and to all his land,"

Wisdom is known by its demonstration of power (Matthew 11:19b). Moses did terrible things in the land of Egypt. He wrought signs and wonders but when he was to impact Joshua, scripture says he transferred wisdom to him and Joshua began to do signs and wonders. In wisdom lies power. The bible says Jesus Christ is the wisdom and the power. Wisdom and power are interwoven. If you claim to be a wise man then you must be a man of signs and wonders. It is not in the ability to give speech.

That is why Paul said that your wisdom should not rest in the ability of man. The power of God is the wisdom of God. When they looked at Jesus, they said what kind of wisdom has this man that signs and wonder are wrought by him. They attributed signs and wonders to the wisdom He carried.

Proverbs 18:1.
"Through desire a man, having separated himself, seeketh and intermeddleth with all wisdom. "

So when a man intermingles himself with all wisdom, it is actually power he intermingles with. There has to be a desire in us to see the dimensions of God's power. We owe the world an encounter with God and we are the ones to give the world that encounter. We are not supposed to explain our powerlessness and give excuses. Jesus said, "behold I give you power to tread upon serpent and scorpion and nothing shall by any means hurt you" (Luke 10:19). He has given you, stop explaining your powerlessness, rather demonstrate his power. The faith you can't demonstrate, you don't have.

Hebrews 11:33.
"Who through faith subdue kingdom, wrought righteousness, obtained promises, and stopped the mouth of lions"

Your faith is proven by the demonstration of power. We must get discontented and stop being average, powerless Christians, because there should be nothing called powerless Christianity. The word 'Christian' means a worker of miracles.

Isaiah 61:1.
"The spirit of the Lord God is upon me; because the Lord hath anointed me to preach good tidings unto the meek; he hath sent me to bind up the brokenhearted, to proclaim liberty to the captives, and the opening of the prison to them that are bound"

The Gospel is Kingdom Power

The gospel is the key to the power of God and that is why an evangelist carries more power than any other office of the five-fold ministry. They understand the secret of power, which is the gospel. What is the gospel? The gospel is that Jesus came to earth; He was crucified on the cross, buried, rose on the third day and ascended into heaven. To declare this is declaring the gospel.

The cross was where the real power was displayed, the cross is the power of God. As such anywhere the cross is, there is power. The gospel is good news; you don't have to be under oppression anymore. When you preach the gospel to someone that is sick and you can't heal the person, it is not the complete gospel. We must occupy and stop wickedness. We must desire and get desperate about this issue before revival can spark up. Our character as Christians should be power. The preaching of the gospel is power (1 Corinthians 4:20).

When a church is reduced to mere words it means it lacks power. Little wonder why some churches are drying up, for only in the day of the Lord's power shall the people shall be willing.

Habakkuk 1:5.
"Behold ye among the heathen, and regard, and wonder marvelously: for I will work a work in your days, which ye will not believe, though it be told you"

The Kingdom is power. We are called to seek the kingdom which means we are to seek power. The act of doing miracles, signs and wonders is actually the kingdom.

1 Corinthians 4:20.
"The kingdom of God is not in words but in power".

You can't claim you have the kingdom and not have power. When we talk about the revelation of Jesus, we are only talking about the wisdom and power of God. There is no excuse for powerlessness.

We are living for a greater purpose. We are in the kingdom for such a time as this. We must affect our surroundings, environment and people around us. We are now forced to fight our battles with physical means because of our lack of power. The church must rise up and begin to work in the wisdom and power of God because that is kingdom and that is Jesus being revealed. We can only draw the world to God through power. We must subdue the earth by the kingdom of God, but this we can only achieve through the wisdom and power of God.

We must bring proofs to our world. Our bodies should be transmitters of the power of God. We must get tired of where we are and get hungry and desperate for greater dimensions of the power of God. We must ask for evidence. The power that raised Jesus dwells inside of you. Power is your spiritual inheritance.

Ephesians 1:18-21.
18. "The eyes of your understanding being enlightened; that ye may know what is the hope of His calling, and what the riches of the glory of His inheritance in the saints,

19. And what is the exceeding greatness of His power to us-ward who believe, according to the working of his mighty power,

20. Which He wrought in Christ, when He raised Him from the dead, and set Him at His own right hand in the heavenly places,

21. Far above all principality, and power, and might, and dominion, and every name that is named, not only in this world, but also in that which is to come."

CHAPTER 2
PENTECOST

Paul said "that I may know Him and the power of His resurrection" (Philippians 3:10). You can't know Him till you are able to comprehend His resurrection because He was not complete until He resurrected. The bible says "for as He is now, so are we" (1 John 4:17). This implies that, before He became who He is now; He had to resurrect from the dead. So, you can't claim you know Him without having a glimpse of the very vital part of His reality which is His resurrection from the dead. The bible says "if we share in His death, we shall also share in His resurrection." Pentecost is not Easter.

Though they occur in the same season; it was Easter that gave birth to Pentecost. There were three major traditions or feasts the Israelites celebrated, and two out of them are very prominent in the season of Easter.

    1. The feast of wheat (Also known as the feast of harvest).

    2. Passover feast.

    3. Feast of Bali.

The feast of harvest is the Pentecost in the New Testament while the Passover was the one in Exodus12:7-13, when they had blood on their lintels which signified a passing over from evil and death.

Exodus 12:7-13.

7. "Then they shall take some of the blood and put it on the two doorposts and the lintel of the houses in which they eat it

8. They shall eat the flesh that night, roasted on the fire; with unleavened bread and bitter herbs they shall eat it

9. Do not eat any of it raw or boiled in water, but roasted, its head with its legs and its inner parts

10. And you shall let none of it remain until the morning; anything that remains until the morning you shall burn

11. In this manner you shall eat it: with your belt fastened, your sandals on your feet, and your staff in your hand. And you shall eat it in haste. It is the LORD's Passover

12. For I will pass through the land of Egypt that night, and I will strike all the firstborn in the land of Egypt, both man and beast; and on all the gods of Egypt I will execute judgments: I am the LORD

13. The blood shall be a sign for you, on the houses where you are. And when I see the blood, I will pass over you, and no plague will befall you to destroy you, when I strike the land of Egypt."

In the New Testament, Christ became our Passover. Apostle Paul caught a glimpse of this reality and gave us an admonition.

1 Corinthians 5:7&8.

"Purge out therefore the old leaven that ye may be a new lump, as ye are unleavened. For even Christ our Passover is sacrificed for us: therefor let us keep the feast, not with old leaven, neither with the leaven of malice and wickedness; but with the unleavened bread of sincerity and truth."

Between the Passover and Pentecost is fifty days. Every celebration of the harvest festival which is called "nabi" marks a new calendar in Israel. This celebration is usually done with all the prominent people in Israel.

Revealing The Person Of Jesus

In reality, there is no such thing as Pentecostal power. It was only a power that came on the day of Pentecost. Pentecost actually means 'fifty'. It's the fiftieth day after the Passover when the Israelites gather for a celebration of the feast of harvest; the harvest of what God has blessed them with.
The Old Testament was Christ concealed, while the New Testament is Christ revealed, so all the while; they were dealing with Jesus but they didn't know. The entire feast was talking about the person of Jesus; He was the fulfillment of those feasts.
He came to earth, died and resurrected on the third day. He didn't need to wait for the fiftieth day before He resurrected. There was a power that resurrected Him and there was also a power that was unleashed on the fiftieth day upon the early Apostles.

Acts 2:1-4.

1. "And when the day of Pentecost was fully come, they were all with one accord in one place.

2. And suddenly there came a sound from heaven as of a rushing mighty wind, and it filled all the house where they were sitting.

3. And there appeared unto them cloven tongues like as of fire, and it sat upon each of them.

4. And they were all filled with the Holy Ghost, and began to speak with other tongues, as the Spirit gave them utterance."

The Pentecostal power actually started on the third day. Jesus said "say ye not, there are four months and then comes the harvest; it is now, the fields are ripe" (John 4:35).
After the feast of harvest He saw the multitudes and said to them "he that thirst let him come."

John 7:37-39.

37. "In the last day, that great day of the feast, Jesus stood and cried, saying, If any man thirst, let him come unto Me, and drink

38. He that believeth on Me, as the scripture hath said, out of his belly shall flow rivers of living water

39. But this spake He of the Spirit, which they that believe on Him should receive: for the Holy Ghost was not yet given; because that Jesus was not yet glorified."

Normally one of the rites carried out during the feast of harvest was the pouring of water on the floor which symbolized rest.

However, they were not having rest, else He wouldn't have made such declaration requesting them to come. Jesus was a combination of all the three feasts in one. The bible says He will give you the former and latter rain in one (Joel 2:23).

Birth of the Joel Generation

Jesus is the fulfillment of all the feasts. The feast of Bali was actually the harvest of the sons of God. He came to raise many sons unto glory (Hebrews 2:10). He died as a seed to bring forth a harvest of sons.

This is actually why we gather during Easter to celebrate. They gathered for the harvest of wheat but we gather for the harvest of sons. Easter is to celebrate what the power of God has done in our individual lives; but this time, not in wheat but in the Holy Ghost.

The bible says they were gathered in the upper room (to raise sons) and the Holy Ghost came down upon them; like wind, fire and they spoke in tongues.

The day of Pentecost is the day you see various activities and operations of the Holy Ghost, and Easter is when we celebrate various dimensions of the spirit.

Joel 2:23-32.

23. "Be glad then, ye children of Zion, and rejoice in the LORD your God: for He hath given you the former rain moderately, and He will cause to come down for you the rain, the former rain, and the latter rain in the first month.

24. And the floors shall be full of wheat, and the fats shall overflow with wine and oil.
25. And I will restore to you the years that the locust hath eaten, the cankerworm, and the caterpiller, and the palmerworm, my grseat army which I sent among you.

26. And ye shall eat in plenty, and be satisfied, and praise the name of the LORD your God, that hath dealt wondrously with you: and my people shall never be ashamed.

27. And ye shall know that I am in the midst of Israel, and that I am the LORD your God, and none else: and my people shall never be ashamed.

28. And it shall come to pass afterward, that I will pour out my spirit upon all flesh; and your sons and your daughters shall prophesy, your old men shall dream dreams, your young men shall see visions:

29. And also upon the servants and upon the handmaids in those days will I pour out my spirit.

30. And I will shew wonders in the heavens and in the earth, blood, and fire, and pillars of smoke.

31. The sun shall be turned into darkness, and the moon into blood, before the great and the terrible day of the LORD come.

32. And it shall come to pass, that whosoever shall call on the name of the LORD shall be delivered: for in mount Zion and in Jerusalem shall be deliverance, as the LORD hath said, and in the remnant whom the LORD shall call."

Joel 2 is a prophetic book. It speaks about the end of the days of the Jews which was brought about by the birthing of a new generation. Joel was prophetically speaking about a combination of seasons. Jesus said "I Am the bread of life" (John 6:35). He was their satisfaction and fulfillment. He was the reason they gathered, the one who came from heaven. God is saying "I want to raise a generation; I want to bring a harvest, not that of wheat but a harvest of people." He came to raise sons unto glory. The bible tells us "they shall be as horse men, they shall run and not be weary, before them is as Eden and behind a desolate place" (Joel 2:1-3). Talking about a generation of men that will do terrible things in righteousness, that will owe no one any apology for the works of God. "Saviors shall come out of Zion" (Obadiah 1.21).

Easter is meant to raise saviors, sons and generals to take over the kingdom. It is an empowerment to go and do more. Joel was trying to explain the old and the new. Pentecost was the Greek word for the feast of harvest and Easter means the celebration of the resurrected life.

God's intention in the New Testament is that when He pours out His spirit, Men shall prophesy (Joel 2:28). The major work of a prophet is to equip the church, so that they can prophesy. Prophecy is not just foretelling; as that is only a fragment of prophecy.

It is declaring by the inspiration of the Holy Spirit the realities in heaven that ought to be taking place in your life now. A prophet bridges the gap between heaven and earth. Everything you see in the book of revelation (the seven spirits of God, lightening, thundering, etc) is to give you a picture of what should be happening on earth, so that the earth will look like heaven. It is a fulfillment of purpose, when everything that happens in heaven begins to happen on earth. A prophet does not necessarily create new things, rather, he unveils what should be in your life now. A prophet helps your sensitivity to align with the purpose of God. The bible says whatever you agree, bind or lose on earth is agreed, bound and loosed in heaven. So when a prophet prophesies accurately according to what he or she is seeing in heaven, the bible says you have the power to change it and that is the purpose of Pentecost.

Power is the ability to cause changes. You have been given the ability to decorate earth with heaven, to make earth look like heaven; but for that to happen, the Spirit has to be poured upon all because even the servants have their parts to play.

Christians have become slaves of prophets; many can't do anything without calling a prophet to check. He is not better than you, the only difference is that he has the ability to peep into heaven. A prophet who is outside the word of God, no matter his accuracy, is not functioning from the right source. Their accuracy doesn't authenticate that they are of God, because, for every purpose of God for the earth, the devil also has a counter purpose for the earth. You are a prophet over your life, whatever you say, happens!

An Empowerment for Change

Pentecost is actually an empowerment. It empowers you to cause a change; a celebration of joy and victory. "And you shall receive power after that the Holy Ghost is come upon you" (Acts 1:8).
The Holy Ghost is the one that gives you that ability to cause change.

Micah 3:8.
"But truly I am full of power by the spirit of the LORD, and of judgment, and of might, to declare unto Jacob his transgression, and to Israel his sin."

The Spirit of God empowers you. What came upon them on the day of Pentecost and also resurrected Jesus on the third day was the Holy Ghost. Pentecost or Easter is a celebration of the Holy Ghost; it should be a time when you reflect and allow the Holy Ghost come upon you in full. Where the Spirit of God is present, what you see is manifestations of power (1Corithians 2:1-4). Power brings an ability to speak languages you never learnt. Power is not a force, it is a manifestation, an ability beyond human strength.
The reason for Pentecost or Easter is to give us mind blowing testimonies, because when power comes, what it does is instant. The entire miracle, signs and wonders come as a manifestation of power.

The effect of the Spirit when He comes is power. The manifestation of the Spirit is to profit all (1 Corinthians 12:7). The purpose of Pentecost is to reveal Jesus in reality to us, to bring about the testimony of Jesus in our lives. We carry something precious in our inside to change the world, but we must wake up to the consciousness that "it is not by might nor by power but by his Spirit". "It is God which worketh in us both to will and to do of His good pleasure" (Philippians 2:13) according to the power that is at work in us (Ephesians 1:19).

Zechariah 4:6.
"Then he answered and spake unto me, saying, This is the word of the LORD unto Zerubabel, Saying, Not by might, nor by power, but by My Spirit, saith the LORD of hosts."

The power within you is meant to change the world and that is the purpose of Easter. God is limited by what is within us. He is eager to heal and do miracles but will you allow Him do that through you.
Easter is a time when we allow God to manifest through us and that is the testimony of Jesus.
The evidence of Jesus in you is that you are enriched with all utterance (1Corinthians1:4-6).
You can say things by the Spirit of God because you have all knowledge, supernaturally, and lack behind in no gift. We don't know you have power, except you manifest (Romans 5:19).

When the Holy Ghost is present in you, there will be manifestations of the gifts of the Spirit (1Corinthians 2:4). A Christian is not known by talking but by impact, through the demonstration of God's Spirit and power that is within him. What you are conscious of, you manifest. Do you know what you carry? Are you conscious of it? Are you manifesting it? You carry something great in you to change the world. We must wake up to this consciousness; we must be sensitive; we must be aligned, connected and allow God to flow through us. Anytime we talk about Jesus, it should be an evidence of what will happen again, for the testimony of Jesus is the spirit of prophecy (Revelation 19:10). There's just a thin line between that problem and your miracle, connect to the flow.

Powerlessness is not an Option

It is Christian-like that power should be a way of life. Being a Christian means Christ resides in you and Christ is the power of God. Powerlessness is not an option or an excuse in Christianity. Once you become born again, you become a man of power. Your encounter with Christ is an encounter with power. The book of Acts is the standard for a basic Christian life; it is the least quality of life a believer should have. Each chapter was an encounter of diverse manifestations of power, to stop the powers of hell.

The church owes the world an encounter with God. The world is waiting for the manifestation of the sons of God (Romans 8:19), those that will manifest the raw power of God on the face of the earth.

In the day of the Lord's power the people shall be willing (Psalms 110:3); so we can compel kingdoms to know God, serve Him and give their all to Him. Power is not an alternative for a Christian; it is not for the minister or a chosen people, it is for the entire believers.

A man who walks in mystery (the power of God) is a man who can manifest God in the flesh on the face of the earth. A generation is coming that will not be bound by religious limitations, a people that have gone beyond the limits of religion. However, this mystery belongs to a certain type of people; those who will hunger beyond the normal.

Even though these mysteries are yours as a believer, if you don't show some level of desire and need for them, you will not access them.

There has to be a hunger and desperation in your spirit for this reality. Paul had access to this power because of his desperate desire. In Philippians 3:10, he said "I count all things as dung that I may know Him and the power of His resurrection", even though Paul had tasted power, he still believed that there were greater realms of power in the mystery of God that he could relate with. One of the inheritances of a believer is power, the bible says "God has not given us the spirit of fear, but He has given to us the spirit of power, love and sound mind". Jesus told the disciples not to leave the upper room until they were endued with power from on high, so power is one of the benefits and inheritance of being a Christian.

Don't be satisfied with the manifestations of people falling under the power of God, there is still more. There are creative powers given to men to call those things that be not as though they were (Romans 4:17).

Proverbs 18:1.
"Through desire a man, having separated himself, seeketh and intermeddleth with all wisdom."

A man had been praying for fourteen years that the cloud of darkness over the city where he lived be moved, but that didn't happen until fourteen years later. He saw in the spirit that the cloud of darkness was moving out, then he asked "Lord, what is the meaning of this?" and God said, "my son Lestra Sumrall is in town". That was a possibility because he had tasted of the power of the age to come; he had been able to access classified information that mortal men couldn't access by reason of his hunger.

He was able to break past natural and spiritual resistances because there is always more for those who are desperate, who will not be satisfied with where they are but press in for more. God is always ready to satisfy those that are hungry but as long as you are not hungry God cannot give to you. There has to be a hunger for more of the power and the Glory of God beyond the normal.

We keep pressing in for power until His enemies become His footstool. The bible says "by terrible things in righteousness shall He answer us" (Psalms 65:5). That scripture can only be fulfilled when raw power comes on earth, and we are that generation that will manifest God's power.

The purpose of this book is to increase your hunger for this reality because without hunger you cannot enter into the realm of power. Jacob was a blessed man by covenant but his life was a mess and he was not fulfilling destiny, He knew something in Him was crying for expression, and as a result, didn't sit down with his wishes, but set himself apart for an encounter with God (Genesis 32:28-30).

CHAPTER 3
THE MYSTERY OF POWER

Life is about the mystery of power, and the sooner you know this, the better so you could function in the authority that belongs to you. The word mystery means something that is from another realm, something that is not available to us, something that is hidden. Mystery makes you exempted from what happens to mortal men.

A mystery is something that is obscure; it is something that you cannot know through your mental exertion. It is a hidden secret though seen but not understood, it is something that is incomprehensible.

A mystery is something you may even hear of in familiar words but cannot decode because there is something beyond what they are saying that also has a form of power and grace beyond what you are seeing. Mysteries are only given to deities and not to mortal men.

A mystery is a secret given to people who have been initiated into a group, it is a classified knowledge. God has initiated you into a close group where you have access into a certain light that makes you walk as God on earth. There are mysteries in the word of God that a believer ought to encounter, so that he can be exempted from certain things that limit mortal men. Godliness is a mystery. No one has ever seen God but God was made manifest in the flesh; that means God can be seen (John 1:14).

I Timothy 3:16.
"And without controversy great is the mystery of godliness: God was manifest in the flesh justified in the Spirit, seen of angels, preached unto the Gentiles, believed on in the world, received up into glory."

God became something we could see and relate with. For the first time they could behold God in the flesh. What a mystery! Your highest level of godliness is seeing God in the flesh. The Bible says …of the things which we have seen, touched and our hands have handled (1John 1:1), that means divinity can be handled.

Colossians 1:26-27.
26. "Even the mystery which hath been hid from ages and from generations, but now is made manifest to his saints:

27. To whom God would make known what is the riches of the glory of this mystery among the Gentiles; which is Christ in you, the hope of glory:"

The power of God which is the mystery of God was something that was concealed from mankind but has now been made manifest to the saints; "Christ in you the Hope of Glory". All Moses had, was a shadow of the main mystery, all Elijah had was also a shadow of the mystery. The bible says they were searching diligently to know what manner of time the main mystery will be revealed (1 Peter 1:11). All they manifested was the outer court experience.

The mysteries of the kingdom have been revealed to the saints but not all have access to these mysteries. Custodians of mysteries are dangerous people. The Bible says they have power to shut the heaven and the earth and nobody can kill them in the day of their prophecy. They have access to the court room of heaven and are connected to a realm beyond the physical.

The power of the age to come is the flow of various dimensions of mysteries and your reasoning faculty cannot give you access to it. It took the resurrected Christ to reveal the gospel to Paul, showing him what happened at Calvary, in the upper room and the breaking of bread. That's why he could say "my gospel." It was not preached to him, it was given to him by revelation.

Power Your Spiritual Inheritance

Power was not a special gift given to you when you got born again but a package that came with your salvation. The kingdom of God is not in words but in power (1 Corinthians 4:20).

So when you became part of Gods kingdom, you became entitled to a life of power (John 1:12). A Christianity void of power is a Christianity void of taste and flavor.

Even the bible admonishes us to turn away from those whose Christianity is void of power (2 Timothy 3:5). The power of God is ever available but God is in search of instruments through which He would convey his power. We must become conscious of this reality, for a man that is in honour and understandeth not, is like a beast that perishes (Psalms 49:20). The bible says you shall lay hands on the sick and they shall recover.

Mark 16:15-18.

15. "And he said unto them, Go ye into all the world, and preach the gospel to every creature.

16. He that believeth and is baptized shall be saved; but he that believeth not shall be damned.

17. And these signs shall follow them that believe; In my name shall they cast out devils; they shall speak with new tongues;

18. They shall take up serpents; and if they drink any deadly thing, it shall not hurt them; they shall lay hands on the sick, and they shall recover."

Why wouldn't God just heal them Himself? He is looking for an instrument of extension.

He wants someone through whom He can manifest this glory. Yes He does the healing but we share the glory because we have become partners with Him. The bible says we are His workmanship... (Ephesians 2:10). Just as we cannot do without God, so also He cannot do without us. If He could, He wouldn't need to use you to heal the sick. Just as we can't do without the angels, so also they can't do without us, because they have limits, and God also has a limitation.

Remember the bible refers to us as the body of Christ. We are his hands to reach out to the world with his very life, his eyes through which he sees the world, his mouth by which he speaks to his creation and his feet to reach out to the ends of the earth.

We are God's extension on earth, conveyors of his very life and dispensers of this life to our sphere of influence. Indeed we owe this world an encounter with God. We owe the world an encounter with his life and power.

Jesus must be seen once again on our streets. Wickedness has prevailed for too long. Cruelty lies in the dark places of the earth (PS 74:20). The lights of the world must arise and take their place. We must refuse the devil from having global fame and making the news via the insurgencies and diverse disasters plaguing nations.

Not on our shift and not in our time. We are in the days of his power. There's going to be a heavy display of power between the kingdom of God and the kingdom of darkness.

Matthew 24:7.
"For nations shall rise against nations and kingdoms against kingdoms..."

There is a place you get to in God that heaven has no choice but to respond to the words that you speak, as though it was God who spoke the words.

1 Kings 17:1.
"And Elijah the Tishbite, who was of the inhabitants of Gilead, said unto Ahab, As the LORD God of Israel liveth, before whom I stand, there shall not be dew nor rain these years, but according to my word."

Elijah didn't say God said there won't be rain but because he stands in God's presence, he could boldly declare that there won't be rain. Men won't serve the prophets of Baal if they didn't have power but one man (Elijah) brought four hundred of them down.

When certain people speak, it is the end of prayers because heaven honours their words. While for some, it is the beginning of prayers. When they prophesy over people's lives, they get attacked.

The ability to command tangible results is a realm of power and the attainment of stature with God. There is a man called David Hogan, as long as he is in a town, nobody dies. He raised over two hundred people from the dead. However, it took hunger and pressing into God to make that dimension a reality, it took him fasting, studying the word and prayer.

Psalms 107:23-24.
"They that go down to the sea in ships, that do business in great waters; These see the works of the Lord, and his wonders in the deep."

In the spiritual realm, your body doesn't matter, it is your spirit. If you don't have stature in the spirit you are useless in the physical. The people witches can kill are those that are feathers—weight, not everybody is "killable". They can only try to frustrate them but can't kill them. When an Angel comes into a meeting and the power of God is present in that meeting, many people still don't go home blessed, not because He's not present, but because the ability to buy things and make them a reality in your life depends on your purchasing power.

Your spiritual sense is your purchasing power, but needs to be utilized. What differentiates men of God is not in the ability to call Jesus, because everybody calls Jesus.

Bishop David Oyedepo stated that calling the name of Jesus once is enough. As a result, your strength is what speaks in the realm of the spirit, the realm responds to men of strength.

Any man that must make impact and walk in dimensions of power must be a man of prayer. He must spend quality time with God in the place of prayer to gain sufficient strength. When you pray, especially in the spirit, you speak the wisdom of God and bring the wisdom of this world to naught.

Whatsoever Satan has done in his own ability and wisdom to bring someone down, when we speak, it will come to naught (1 Corinthians 2:5-18). Anytime you pray in the Holy Ghost, you are praying to God and compelling mysteries that give instruction to the ability and power of God to bring them into action.

Proofs of Kingdom Power

1.   God's Acts of Love

Christ came to live an exemplary life. He was an epitome of how the Christian life should look like. Every day of His life was power, power and power. He healed the sick and changed nature. However, every power he demonstrated was to advance the course of humanity, to tell them that God cared for them. Power is to make us and the world see the ability and love of God towards us.

Matthew 14:14.
"And Jesus went forth, and saw a great multitude, and was moved with compassion toward them and he healed their sick."

Without power you cannot function, you are not an effective Christian if you don't have power. I get surprised when Christians are without power and they are okay. What is your gospel? What are you telling the world? There is no difference between you and the unbeliever out there. We are not called to comfort people by telling them God will do it, we are called to solve problems. We are called to reveal the God we carry in us. It doesn't do anybody any good if we die without unlocking the God inside of us. God is looking for kingdom men who will hold a city to ransom, not allowing demonic men hold sway. Let's get to a point that we can compel a generation to seek after God because somebody is able to hold sickness and disease to ransom and command them to get out. Demons should be giving testimonies that they escaped the assault of a child of God and not the other way round.

If you can prove that your God can do better than the god the world serves, they will serve him. Jacob wrestled with God, so much so that even the Angel acknowledged that he had power with both God and man.

Ephesians 2:1, 2.
1. "And you hath He quickened, who were dead in trespasses and sins;

2. Wherein in time past ye walked according to the course of this world, according to the prince of the power of the air, the spirit that now worketh in the children of disobedience:"

Your salvation began from power. It was a manifestation of power. Anyone who says that Christianity is not all about power is the greatest liar on earth. Christianity is all about power, because you became born again by the power of God, and you can't remain a Christian except by the same power. Christianity can be defined as the reality of power. That is why when anyone gets born again, he can't continue in sin because of the power at work in him.

1 Thessalonians 1:5.
"For our gospel came not unto you in word only, but also in power and in the HolyGhost, and in much assurance..."

Have you not been amazed at the change of certain individual after they experience salvation? The bible says the mad man of "Gadara" was chained with many chains, yet he could break them. He never thought he could be okay. But when Jesus came along, a man carrying the atmosphere of power, he became another man (Mark 5:1-20).

2.   Custodians of the Earth

God will hold us accountable for whatever happens in the earth realm. We are to be held responsible for the prevailing insurgencies in nations, oppressions upon individuals and families, deaths and sicknesses ravaging millions all over the world. The bible says the heavens belong to God but the earth He has given to men (Psalms 115:16). A good picture of God's reactions when the custodians of the earth fail to carry out their obligations, are captured in Psalms 82.

Psalms 82:1-8.
1. "God standeth in the congregation of the mighty; he judgeth among the gods.

2. How long will ye judge unjustly, and accept the persons of the wicked? Selah.

3. Defend the poor and fatherless: do justice to the afflicted and needy.

4. Deliver the poor and needy: rid them out of the hand of the wicked.

5 . They know not, neither will they understand; they walk on in darkness: all the foundations of the earth are out of course.

6. I have said, ye are gods; and all of you are children of the most High.

7. But ye shall die like men, and fall like one of the princes.

8. Arise, O God, judge the earth: for thou shalt inherit all nations."

We have been entrusted with a kingdom mandate of enforcing God's will on earth, in order to make the earth look like heaven (Matthew 6:10). Every transformation plunders hell. Every miracle terminates the works of the devil (1 John 3:8). Our desperate conditions are taken care of by every encounter with God.

3.	A Light In Darkness

The original flame of Pentecost, the Holy Spirit Himself, burns within my soul (Acts 1:8). I have a promise from God. I am a part of a new breed of people - "the remnant" destined to do greater works than Jesus did in His earthly ministry (John 14:12).
It seems so difficult to see the Church with substantial influence and impact in these last days. It was God who purposed that the bride should be spotless and without wrinkle (Ephesians 5:27). It was God who declared, "Behold darkness will cover the earth but His glory will appear upon you (Isaiah 60:2)".
We are the triumphant Church. In these days, God has strategically placed us in the darkest situations to demonstrate His sovereignty.
The dark circumstances of the world become the stage upon which He displays His glorious Church! Where sin abounds, grace abounds much more (Romans 5:20).

4.	Transmitters of the Supernatural

God wants to raise a special breed of people through whom He will manifest His glory upon the earth.
The great Apostle Paul was so filled with the power of God that beyond the miracles wrought by physical contact with him, handkerchiefs and aprons taken from his body had enough potency and virtue to heal the sick. So his hands did miracles and his body also conveyed it.

Acts 19:11-12.
11. "God wrought special miracles through the hands of the Paul

12. So that from his body were brought unto the sick handkerchiefs or aprons, and the diseases departed from them, and the evil spirits went out of them."

Jesus also said in his encounter with the woman with the issue of blood (for twelve years) "virtues went out of me (Luke 8:46)". That means He was a carrier of something. Power is not meant to be in heaven, it is meant to be contained in man and conveyed through man.

Your body was wired up to carry power. Jesus' body, which was his earthly suit, was a conveyor and a carrier of power. The Bible says when He went to preach the gospel of the kingdom, He was healing the sick and cleansing the leper. You are a carrier of power, as such, can reproduce the works of Jesus and even do greater.

1 Peter 1:3.
"Blessed be the God and Father of our Lord Jesus Christ, which according to His abundant mercy hath begotten us again unto a lively hope by the resurrection of Jesus Christ from the dead."

What we were brought into, was as a result of His resurrection. No wonder Paul said "that I may know Him and the power of His resurrection (Philippians 3:10)." Your salvation is actually a by-product of a working power. Colossians 1:13 says you were translated from the kingdom of darkness into the kingdom of God. It was a contention of power. The bible says the world is under bondage, not willingly, but by the power of he that subjected it in hope (Romans 8:20). So, there is a power that compels a man to remain in the state of bondage. It takes a higher power to save man. It says He has begotten us by the resurrection of Jesus Christ from the dead, so there is a power called the power of resurrection by which He begot you. If power did all these, then it is power that can also sustain you from being taken back to where you were delivered from, and this power need not be wakened again.

When you speak in tongues you unravel the mystery of Christ within you which is meant for your Glory. Speaking in tongues is speaking power. Speaking in tongue is instructing angels. You are instructing the realm of God's glory to have dominion over the natural realm. When you speak in tongues you cause the mystery of God and his power in you to prevail. To walk in power, is to learn to speak in tongues always. Speaking it without this consciousness deprives you of the power available to you. It is a language that exists in the realm of God which He gave you to enable you function in His realm. It is a tool to bring down what's in His realm.

1 Corinthians 14:2.
"For he that speaketh in an unknown tongue speaketh not unto men, but unto God: for no man understandeth him; howbeit in the spirit he speaketh mysteries."

Tongues are the language of the power of the age to come. So for you to be able to draw from the power of the age to come, you need the language of the age to come. When you speak in tongues, you are drawing from the dimensions of Glory.

A man in Zaria (Kaduna state) once said, if given the blood samples of believers for analysis, he could detect who speaks in tongues among them and who doesn't without being told. He affirms that there's a kind of life in their blood, because when you speak in tongues you are drawing life and incubating life.

Anytime you speak in tongues you are speaking his word and you amass wealth of power. I've never seen a believer who speaks in tongues and is held bound by demons, except the person is praying from his mind.

Anytime I use God's language, it commands angels, because you are saying what he says as it was He who gave you the language. When you speak in tongues, you connect to the mind of God, it is not as though you command God but you come into alignment with what is in his mind. So He sees someone that will agree with Him. It's like making a way for Him to act.

When you pray in tongues, you gain stature with God. When you pray too long outside, it shows that you have not done your homework. Let your word count when you speak. Whatever is made from dust submits to the supernatural.

A genuine child of God should never be satisfied when he is not living in the reality of who He is. It is abnormal for a new creation believer to walk without power because the drive for the impossible is embedded in his DNA. Everything available for the believer who will learn to access the power he has in God because he can walk and work in the reality of all that exist in God. The tool of access is tongues; praying in the Holy Ghost.

5.   Surrounded By Angels

Whenever you leave your home, you leave with power, as you sleep, you sleep in power. Everything you do as a child of God is sustained in power. You are surrounded with angels that carry power.
Even the angels around you can't do without power, and if you really have them, it is enough conviction that you carry power.

Matthew 18:10.
"Take heed that ye despise not one of these little once; for I say unto you, that in heaven their angels do always behold the face of my father which is in heaven."

You didn't lose your angels as an adult (Acts 12:15), the difference is that you have not been connected to power through the gospel. The power of God, through the activity of angels broke the power of sin binding a believer and brought about his or her salvation. The bible records that the mad man of "Gadara" came to his senses, though demons suspended his senses and took over his being (Ephesians 2:2), his contact with Jesus (Power) restored it. Do not attack your brothers who have submitted to their flesh but apply wisdom.
Bind the power behind their actions. Remember Peter in the bible, Jesus had to rebuke the Satan in him, not him directly, because there was a power responsible for his actions.

Kenneth Hagin told the story of a very stingy church where he had preached, he said they must be convinced by scriptures, as evidence for giving before they could ever give. In a particular service, Kenneth Hagin told the pastor not to preach about offering but to just ask them to give, and when he did, he recorded an amount he had not received in many years. Anxious to know the secret behind this change, the host minister asked Kenneth Hagin and Kenneth said he saw a demon of stinginess and covetousness over the congregation, which he rebuked, and that led to the result they recorded that day.

CHAPTER 4
THE MYSTERY OF POWER

The bible says "ye shall receive power, after the Holy Ghost is come upon you: and ye shall be my witnesses. (Acts 1:8)". The Holy Ghost is the giver of power. He is the custodian of power. He is the release of power. The three reasons why the Holy Ghost came are to convict the world of sin, of righteousness and of judgment because the prince of this world is judged.

John 16:7-11.
7. "Nevertheless I tell you the truth; It is expedient for you that I go away: for if I go not away, THE COMFORTER will not come unto you; but if I depart, I will send him unto you.

8. And when he is come, he will reprove the world of SIN, and of RIGHTEOUSNESS, and of JUDGMENT:
9. Of SIN, because they believe not on me;

10. Of RIGHTEOUSNESS, because I go to my Father, and ye see me no more;

11. Of JUDGMENT, because the prince of this world is judged."

The Holy Ghost will do again what He had done in Christ. I was, through the Holy Ghost there when Christ healed the sick, raised the dead and manifested the power of God.

Acts 10:38.
38. "How God anointed Jesus of Nazareth with the Holy Ghost and with power: who went about doing good, and healing all that were oppressed of the devil; for God was with him."

He was the power that was manifested. The Holy Ghost shall make you a witness of Christ, which means you, shall duplicate what was done when Christ was here and even more. So in case you have never healed the sick you have the Holy Ghost who has healed the sick, if you have never raised the dead before, don't worry the power that raised Jesus Christ from the dead dwells in you; so there is power to resurrect when you have the Holy Ghost inside you. The first realm of power I want to talk about is the judgmental power.

The Spirit of Judgment

The Holy Ghost is a judgmental Spirit. Power is known to be complete when there is a judgmental part of it. Whether you like it or not, there is a power that wants to oppose you, that is the power of darkness which you were pulled out from. Satan is mad about your salvation because he is already judged. That is why God has given you all authority over serpents and scorpions, over all powers and nothing can hurt you (Luke 10:19). You have power over the works of the enemy and that power is a judgmental power.

Isaiah 54:17.

17. "No weapon that is formed against thee shall prosper; and every tongue that shall rise against thee in JUDGMENT thou shalt condemn. This is the heritage of the servants of the LORD, and their righteousness is of me, saith the LORD."

You have been given the power to condemn and to judge everything. No matter the kind of weapon that is forged against you it won't prosper and every tongue that rises against you, you shall condemn.

Psalms 149:6-9.

6. "Let the high praises of God be in their mouth, and a twoedged sword in their hand;

7. To execute vengeance upon the heathen, and punishments upon the people;

8. To bind their kings with chains, and their nobles with fetters of iron;

9. To execute upon them the JUDGMENT WRITTEN: this honour have all his saints. Praise ye the LORD."

The judgmental power is an inherent power within you. Anytime the enemy rages and boasts don't be afraid; you have the judgmental power to bring him down, David came before Goliath in the Name of the Lord. Don't be afraid of whatever is standing before you. Whosoever shall say unto this mountain be cast into the sea, by judgment and by the power within him, shall have what he says (mark 11:23). Don't remain silent. Use your words.

Words are conveyors of power. The bible says, the words that I speak unto you they are spirit and life (John 6:63). God has given you the two edged sword to execute judgment but if you don't have power you can't execute judgment.

Those that understand the supernatural realm, whether demonic or Godly know that words are conveyors of power. The good news is that no matter what they say, the bible says thou shall condemn it. However, until you condemn it, it remains active.

People that judge are the ones that have been empowered to judge. The reason you have remained where you are is because you have not let your mouth loose to judge.

If you keep quiet, Satan will keep moving in your life and you will remain where you are.

1 Peter 5:8.

8. "Be sober, be vigilant; because your adversary the devil, as a roaring lion, walketh about, seeking whom he may devour:

9. Whom resist stedfast in the faith, knowing that the same afflictions are accomplished in your brethren that are in the world."

A closed mouth is a closed life and a closed destiny. Even if you have been called to enjoy good life, Satan will continue to do bad things in your life because you don't know how to release words of Judgement. You have to release words.

Psalms 149:6-7.
6. "Let the high praises of God be in their MOUTH and a two edged sword in their hand;

7. To execute vengeance upon the heathen, and punishments upon the people;"

Someone practicing witchcraft can speak negative words against you because they understand their standing and the power of words.

A pastor can use negative words against a member and such words will come to pass because there is a level of authority and influence he has in the realm of the spirit. A pastor that curses a member because the member left him or made him angry is an unregenerate pastor. Some pastors consult some demonic things because they want to manifest power, they also do terrible things but those things work against the members. When you sit under such pastors, your destiny is locked up and comes to them while you remain where you are. When they curse you it works because you believe them and your spirit is open to them. Anybody who puts fear in you is not of God. No pastor should conjure words against a member but bless him and let him go.

Enforce Judgment

No weapon formed against you shall prosper because the prince of this world is judged. You have power to release and enforce their judgment and execute their written judgment. They are already condemned but you must enforce their condemnation by the power of your words. It is better witches dream of you pursuing them and not the other way round. Jesus said "Get thee behind me, Satan: thou art an offence unto me: for thou savourest not the things that be of God, but those that be of men" (Matthew 16:23). You have to be authoritative and bold for fear has torment.

I John 4:18.
18. "There is no fear in love; but perfect love casteth out fear: because FEAR HATH TORMENT. He that feareth is not made perfect in love."

People do deliverance with fear in their hearts. This is an anomaly. The bible says "nothing shall by any means hurt you." So on no account shall you permit Satan to have his way in your life, family or domain. Any demon that violates the scripture is allowed to be condemned. God allows some things to come your way not because you are not prayerful enough but because you are not using your right as a child of God. He sometimes uses such situations to train you; champions are trained in the ring.

1 Corinthians 10:13.
"There hath no temptation taken you but such as is common to man: but God is faithful, who will not suffer you to be tempted above that ye are able; but will with the temptation also make a way to escape, that ye may be able to bear it."

When God allows some circumstances come your way, it is not because He wants to destroy you or because He doesn't care. Anytime you pray and you don't get the answer, it means that God wants to use you to bring about the answer.

He is depending on you. Moses cried to God to release His power and God asked Moses "what is in your hands"? He was telling him that I have been delivering you but now I want to deliver through you.

Anytime you pray to God to heal someone and that person doesn't get healed, it may be because God wants to heal that person through you. God wants to partner with you. Every pharaoh in your life is not your problem (Romans 9:17); that uncle in the village that is controlling the family is not your problem.

The reason God allowed that uncle to be alive till you were born is because God wants to use you to destroy him. You are dealing with spirits without bodies, and except you judge that power, it remains the way it is. So anytime there is a storm and you have prayed and God allowed the storm it is because He wants to glorify Himself. That situation has lingered because you have not done anything about it.

Now is the time to do something about it to end that problem. The reason why the enemy is throwing you anyhow is because they have not seen the judgmental power being manifested through you, when they see fire, they will leave you alone. There is a power to execute judgment and God has raised you up to destroy the works of the devil. Anytime there is no encounter with the power of God Christianity becomes mere religion. In exchange of the power of God we bring entertainment to the church, and demons are having a good day. If there is no power in the church it is not the church of God.

1 Corinthians 2:4-5.
4. "And my speech and my preaching was not with enticing words of man's wisdom, but in demonstration of the Spirit and of power:

5. That your faith should not stand in the wisdom of men, but in the power of God."

We are not called to debate in eloquence but to manifest the raw power of God. Until you are angry enough you can't be free enough.

A child of God can be in a place and judge evil or wickedness in another place without being physically present. The church has the power to deliver someone to Satan to destroy the flesh if the person continues in an unrepentant act, so that the spirit may be saved.

1Corinthians 5:1-5.
1. "It is reported commonly that there is fornication among you, and such fornication as is not so much as named among the Gentiles, that one should have his father's wife.

2.   And ye are puffed up, and have not rather mourned, that he that hath done this deed might be taken away from among you.

3. For I verily, as absent in body, BUT PRESENT IN SPIRIT, HAVE JUDGED ALREADY, as though I were present, concerning him that hath so done this deed,

4. In the name of our Lord Jesus Christ, when ye are gathered together, and my spirit, with the power of our Lord Jesus Christ

,
5. To deliver such an one unto Satan for the destruction of the flesh, that the spirit may be saved in the day of the Lord Jesus."

The church has the power to judge, it is not a weakling, it is not a place for failures, it is a place where champions are raised. There are two books in heaven; one for salvation and the other for our works which is our reward system. If you don't manifest the power of God given to you, there will be no reward for you in heaven. That means our reward in heaven is not the same. God loves to see you demonstrate his power.

He wants the church to wake up in power. For a true church in power, Satan is a servant to them. The church is a place of violent men who can turn the world upside down, men who will subdue kingdoms, men who will wrought righteousness, men who will shut the mouths of lions and men who will turn aliens to flight. Judge everything that is not of God around you.
You are not a prayer project, refuse to be one. The power within you is a super power, it's the power of the age to come.

Destroy the Works of the Devil

We have been entrusted with the kingdom mandate of executing God's judgment on the earth realm. Wickedness is not permitted to prevail around us. We are the stoppers of lawlessness on earth.

Acts 13:6-12.
6." And when they had gone through the isle unto Paphos, they found a certain sorcerer, a false prophet, a Jew, whose name was Barjesus:

7. Which was with the deputy of the country, Sergius Paulus, a prudent man; who called for Barnabas and Saul, and desired to hear the word of God

8. But Elymas the sorcerer (for so is his name by interpretation) withstood them, seeking to turn away the deputy from the faith.

9. Then Saul, (who also is called Paul,) filled with the Holy Ghost, set his eyes on him,

10. And said, O full of all subtilty and all mischief, thou child of the devil, thou enemy of all righteousness, wilt thou not cease to pervert the right ways of the Lord?

11. And now, behold, THE HAND OF THE LORD IS UPON THEE, and thou shalt be blind, not seeing the sun for a season. And immediately there fell on him a mist and a darkness; and he went about seeking some to lead him by the hand.

12. Then the deputy, when he saw what was done, believed, being astonished at the doctrine of the Lord."

The hand of God is the power of God and He has given the church that power to stop the works of the devil, but instead of manifesting power, we are raising psychologists. When someone is under the power of demons, we say it is a psychological problem. No therapy can work when a demon is present. You don't medicate demons, you cast them out. Whatever has a spiritual origin cannot be handled using physical methods. Believers are faced with some oppositions greater than them, because they have not walked in their authorities. God has not given you a spirit of fear but the spirit of power and that power is the Holy Ghost. I love it when someone is smoking, you lay hands on him and instantly, he loses the desire to smoke.

That is real power, because it is a demon that is responsible for that action. Don't counsel the smoker to try to gradually reduce his smoking habit little by little by taking a cigarette per day instead of three. When a habit persists, it's an indication that a demon has taken an advantage of your ignorance. In no time, you will come under the control of that habit and can only be liberated when you have judged that demon. Jesus judged sickness, He judged oppression (Acts 10:38). Whatever has a spiritual origin can only be dealt with using supernatural power.

The bible calls sickness an unclean spirit but as generations went by, people gave different names to it. When there is problem in the home and a demon is behind it they call it issues and the next thing they go for is counseling. When someone cannot control his body, it is a sign of a demonic spirit in operation, so you have to apply the judgmental power, not counseling. Whatever you accept from the doctor, whatever you see and believe becomes your reality.

In heaven there is no sickness, there is no disease, no pain. That pain you feel is an oppression. When there is chaos and fight in the home, there is something behind it, judge it. When the church began to manifest power none dared to join them, everybody became afraid of them because they were a church of power. There are times that Satan begs his demons not to go near certain children of God. The world must see the power of God manifested, as we execute judgment.

Build Up Strength

Ephesians 3:16.
"That he would grant you, according to the riches of his glory, to be strengthened with might by his Spirit in the inner man."

There are certain things that will come your way which God will not stop, not because He wants to kill you, but because He believes in you. What will make you become a true display of what the bible has said about you being far above principalities and powers is the strength you carry. Every child of God, even in his sleep, is bigger than satan. Strength talks about a greater dimension of the supernatural. We are configured for this, created unto good works. It's our destiny, it's our assignment. Going to heaven is your destiny but bringing heaven down is your assignment.

The Apostles went out with boldness after praying in the Holy Ghost and that boldness is the strength which was generated in prayers. God believes in you because He knows what He has placed in you. Explore the strength of God in you.

Your prayer point should be Lord, strengthen me so that when I talk, my voice will cause ripple effects in the realm of the spirit. You only transact business in the spirit through your inner man.

Judges 16:28-30.
"And Samson called unto the Lord, and said, O Lord God, remember me, I pray thee, and strengthen me, I pray thee, only this once, O God, that I may be at once avenged of the Philistines for my two eyes. And Samson took hold of the two middle pillars upon which the house stood, and on which it was borne up, of the one with his right hand, and of the other with his left. And Samson said, Let me die with the Philistines. And he bowed himself with all his might; and the house fell upon the lords, and upon all the people that were therein. So the dead which he slew at his death were more than they which he slew in his life."

Even Samson knew that the human strength couldn't stand in the day of adversity. If you are not strong, witches will use you for pepper soup. The day they touch you in your dream and you pray, they'll leave you for three days then come back again to feed you in the dream. If you fail in the days of adversity it shows the degree of strength you have.

Proverbs 24:10.
"If thou faint in the day of adversity, thy strength is small."

People have vowed not to live immoral lives but when they fall into it they get shocked. Immorality is more spiritual than physical, if you don't have strength, you will fall. For some, when they are about to get a breakthrough, what Satan brings their way is immorality and when they fall into it, they miss that breakthrough. For such a person, all he needs is strength in that area by the anointing.

Psalms 92:10.
"But my horn shalt thou exalt like the horn of an unicorn: I shall be anointed with fresh oil."

The anointing strengthens you and makes you perform like God; it makes you perform with the strength of God.

2 Chronicles 26:15.
"And he made in Jerusalem engines, invented by cunning men, to be on the towers and upon the bulwarks, to shoot arrows and great stones withal. And his name spread far abroad; for he was marvelously helped, till he was strong."

Luke 22:31-32.
"And the Lord said, Simon, Simon, behold, Satan hath desired to have you, that he may sift you as wheat: But I have prayed for thee, that thy faith fail not: and when thou art converted, strengthen thy brethren."

Sometimes, when we go through attacks, the first thing we do easily is warfare, but why were we attacked? Satan attacks you because he feels you are not strong and therefore wants to size your strength. Greater than warfare is strength because warfare is a display of strength. If you have been fighting a case for over ten years, it shows you need strength. Once you are strengthened by God, you take charge of every area of your life.

Philippians 4:13.
"I can do all things through Christ which strengtheneth me."

The word (Christ) means the anointing and we have different kinds of anointing. We have seven Spirits and they have different types of anointing and different types of dimension. You can do all things through Christ (The Anointing) which strengthens you.

If I can bask in a certain anointing enough to get the strength in that anointing, I'll be able to do more with that anointing. Samson prayed and asked God to strengthen him for one last time that he may avenge his enemies. Some people are gifted in raising the dead, it doesn't just fall like that. It's either by an encounter, by impartation or remaining in an environment that produces it. Joshua carried the anointing of Moses because he stayed behind more than the others who left, by so doing, he was strengthening himself in that anointing.

CHAPTER 5
POWER OF THE AGE TO COME

The Christian walk is not for speculations, it is for you to join those that have tasted of the powers of the age to come. There are two kinds of people: those that make things happen and those that watch things happen. Men that have turned the world upside down have the identity of those who make things happen anywhere they go; they are part of the hallmark of fame in heaven and have shaken territories for God (Hebrews 11:33-34).

Hebrews 6:4-5.

4. "For it is impossible for those who were once enlightened, and have tasted of the heavenly gift, and were made partakers of the Holy Ghost

5. And have tasted the good word of God, and the powers of the world to come."

These men have tasted of something higher and they won't settle for anything lower, there is a higher life. Christ did not come to the world only to save you from sin He needed to do that, to get you to His original purpose because sin took us away from God's former intention.

So he had to save us from sin, to bring us back to God's intention for man, that's why he said, have dominion, have power, rule and control. Man is an embodiment of power being. When God's breath came into man, He gave man power over the earth, so man had a territory he was controlling and exercising dominion and power over (Genesis 1:26). Man is a supernatural being who has been given supernatural abilities to demonstrate power over the earth, that is why there is a craving in man to rule. After the fall, man reduced his potentials to his natural abilities. He could not control the earth again because when he sinned, he lost power over the earth.

The power of the age to come is not the power within the realms of the earth; the power within the realms of the earth stays within the laws of the earth but the power of the age to come is beyond the earth realm.

Power beyond the Earth Realm

All the power available in the earth can destroy the earth, but it is still limited when compared to the power of the age to come. In a fallen state, man still explores.

That's why God said "lets drive Adam from the garden lest he comes in contact with a higher power (Genesis 3:22)". All the powers you see today are still the powers of the fallen man, so if Adam had accessed the higher power, it would have been more dangerous.

Christ did not die to raise a weak church, he died to raise a strong church that is not to be persecuted and killed like chickens. If Jesus only reason for coming to earth was to die for your sins, He wouldn't have spent three and a half years on earth. He would have just come and die, go back to heaven and we would be redeemed but that was not the only purpose for which He came. His purpose was what He spent three and a half years doing, showing man what would be restored to him when he is connected back to God. So for three and a half years, He displayed power that has never been seen.

The power of the age to come is a power beyond the physical abilities; it is not within the power of man, even with his great wisdom and knowledge.

It is a power beyond the dimensions of the earth. The power we see today is not the power that Christ delivered to the Church.

Power Over Time and Nature

Peter also craved for power so much, that he wanted to walk on water and he did. If your power doesn't give you supremacy over nature then it is not the power of God. You can't talk about how Peter doubted except you have manifested a higher dimension of power over nature. Jesus didn't give you less power than what He had. He gave you an equal level of power He operated in. Adam had power over nature but when he fell, he became subject to nature.

God made man the crown of His creation, that's why the bible says "what is man that you are mindful of him or the son of man that thou visit him and crown him with Glory and Honour" (Psalms 8:5-6). Adam had not explored the depth of what he was carrying before he fell and that's why we don't have enough testimony about what Adam did. He was too quick to fall into sin. A man, in scripture who was on a divine assignment had eternity opened for him, such that he commanded the sun and moon to stand still.

Joshua 10:12-13.

12. "Then spake Joshua to the LORD in the day when the LORD delivered up the Amorites before the children of Israel, and he said in the sight of Israel, Sun, stand thou still upon Gibeon; and thou, Moon, in the valley of Ajalon.

13. And the sun stood still, and the moon stayed, until the people had avenged themselves upon their enemies. Is not this written in the book of Jasher? So the sun stood still in the midst of heaven, and hasted not to go down about a whole day."

We know scientifically that it's not the sun that moves round the earth. Some things are hidden from us until light hits us. Light gets you angry and provokes the supernatural. Joshua actually told the earth to stand still because it is the earth that moves round the sun and moon. Scientifically, if something stands still, there will be a shaking, but when Joshua spoke to the earth to stand still, there was no sign or record of a crack. He spoke to the earth to stop as though it was not under time and duress. Everything came at a standstill, yet, there was no collision of things. Joshua stopped time and stopped the earth from rotating. If you can stop time you are a master over earth. Joshua exhibited a power that Adam was supposed to have commanding the earth to a standstill. Jesus commanded Lazarus to come forth after he had died for four days and when he came out there was no sign of decay; it was as though it never happened.

Jesus reversed time. The power God gave to the church is not just a power to get drunk and get slain in the spirit, it is the power to reverse time and be able to speak to nature to stand still.

Power for Exploits

When the Apostles prayed in the book of Acts, the building shook (Acts 4:31). The power they received was an earth shaking power; a power to shake the earth and spread the news of Jesus abroad. The power of God is a natural announcer; it has the ability to announce you without effort. It was the power that spread the news of Jesus and his Apostles abroad and itt was the same power that gave the Apostles favour all-round. The book of acts is the least standard we should have as a church. It was the power of the age to come. In the book of Acts, it killed Ananias and Saphirra for lying (Acts 5:3-5). This same power was able to go past prison gates and brought Peter out by causing the prison doors to opened on their own accord(Acts 12:7-10).
The church is not carrying power because it is unable to bring down negative governments. Getting slained in the Spirit is just a sign that you have been qualified to walk in power, yet people have built ministries on the fact that someone fell under the power of God.
That realm of power is just a gate into the power of the age to come. Power is when you can change a case of thirty eight years just like the Apostles did. Any power that you have to do long prayers and fasting to generate in order to solve a healing or demonic case is not the real power.

The power of the age to come is a commanding power. It is an authoritative power and it is the power that is able to change situations.
The power of the age to come does not negotiate with demons or counsel a possessed person. Bodiless beings can't be medicated; they are to be cast out. The power we are talking about is the influence of the age to come on our age. It is the influence of God's ability over our weaknesses. Elisha asked Elijah for a double portion of his Spirit and Elijah said until he saw him being taken up before he could have it. Elisha saw the source of Elijah's power. He saw chariots of fire and a whirlwind which was the dimension Elijah operated from. The power of the age to come is bringing heaven on earth.

Power for Kingdom Influence

Power is bringing the influence of heaven upon earth. It is coming into a realm that is beyond our normal realm. As a child of God, you have power over nature, time and wicked government because power has to do with influence and influence is territorial.

If your power doesn't change a place it is not power. The bible is our standard for the demonstration of the power of God just as it was in the book of acts. Creation is crying for the manifestation of sons because creation has been subject to time and bondage.

Romans 8:19.
19. "For the earnest expectation of the creature waiteth for the manifestation of the sons of God."

Rise up as triumphant beings and begin to speak to sickness, poverty and disease. Begin to speak to curses and change them to blessings. It doesn't matter how long such evil pronouncement has been, for you have the ability to reverse time. Whatever you have suffered because of the family you came from, by the power of God I reverse it and because you are in the kingdom of God, the thing that affected others in your family cannot affect you. The Power of the age to come is to turn away reproaches and make the devil look like he doesn't exist.

There is coming a generation that will rule over the world as though Satan doesn't exist and that generation is here. You were given power by the Holy Ghost to act. So it's time to write the book of your acts.

That you are suffering from a witch is a proof that you are very powerless. If you are suffering from someone that has been defeated then you are very powerless. If a witch comes to oppress your baby at night then you are very powerless.

Psalms 62:11.

11. "God hath spoken once; twice have I heard this; that power belongeth unto God."

Our declaration of power in God is not an empty boast. The power of the witches is a fallen power. Witches manifest their power at night but the children of God have power over the day and over the night. Let's cry for the real thing, that our lives will not be a deviation from the book of Acts.

We have the same Holy Ghost that they had; we don't have a junior Holy Ghost. The Apostles manifested the same thing that Christ manifested.

The power we received in Acts 1:8 is not the power to overcome sin; the power to overcome sin is the one we received when we got born again. When you received Jesus you received power because the bible calls Jesus Christ the wisdom and the power of God.

Some men carry a dimension of power that when they get to a place, kilometers away, sicknesses start disappearing and the dead are brought back to life, power like it was in the Azusa street revival, which was able to take sin out of a land.

Where people stopped committing sin and the police stations were not having criminal cases because of the availability of the power that removed sin from a city.

In Spokane, the power to remove sickness from an entire city was made manifest by John. G. Lake.

CHAPTER 6
THE POWER OF IMMORTALITY

One of the powers of the age to come is the power over death. The only thing that makes you invincible on earth is that death cannot swallow you and that can best be called immortality. Immortality means you are no longer subject to death. The life you received when you became born again is a power of immortality. There is a possibility of living forever and the fact that you don't see it work now does not mean it does not exist.

Genesis 3:22.
22. *"And the LORD God said, Behold, the man is become as one of us, to know good and evil: and now, lest he put forth his hand, and take also of the tree of life, and eat, and LIVE FOR EVER."*

Every reality that exists in the heavenly is a reality that the believer can enjoy on earth. Don't limit your lives to the beliefs of men; let the word of God become your standard. Don't let your life's experience determine your walk with God.
The word of God is the platform for your walk with God. The word mortal means "doomed to death" Adam was supposed to live forever but because of sin, God put him out of the garden. God was not against Adam living forever but at that state, if he lived forever, there will be a problem. God didn't keep the tree in the garden to stop man from living forever. He put it in the garden so that man could live forever but not as a corrupted being.

2 Corinthians 15:49-54.
49. *"And as we have borne the image of the earthy, we shall also bear the image of the heavenly.*

50. *Now this I say, brethren, that flesh and blood cannot inherit the kingdom of God; neither doth corruption inherit incorruption.*

51. *Behold, I shew you a mystery; We shall not all sleep, but we shall all be changed,*

52. *In a moment, in the twinkling of an eye, at the last trump: for the trumpet shall sound, and the dead shall be raised incorruptible, and we shall be changed.*

53. *For this corruptible must put on incorruption, and this mortal must put on immortality.*

54. *So when this corruptible shall have put on incorruption, and this mortal shall have put on immortality, then shall be brought to pass the saying that is written, Death is swallowed up in victory."*

Whatever you get in life is what you settled for. Paul was brought before the Romans because of his message of resurrection. He believed that death was not final and suffered persecution because of his belief.
Death is not final for a believer.

The immortal life was the life that God breathed into Adam but Adam lost that immortal life when he sinned. It was the life in him that was sustaining the dust he was made of. The power of life in you is the one that sustains your mortal body not your blood.

Romans 8:11.

11. "But if the Spirit of him that raised up Jesus from the dead dwell in you, he that raised up Christ from the dead shall also quicken your mortal bodies by his Spirit that dwelleth in you."

If somehow you are involved in an accident you cannot die, the spirit will quicken the cells of your body back to its normal state. The Spirit in you gives life to your mortal body. The bible says there are many who won't see death until the Son of man comes back in power (Mark 9:1).Adam became immortal when God breathe on him and he became a living spirit consequently.

As long as that life was in Adam, the body could not die. The life in you was not created; it was the body that was created. The life in you is God's breath. It's an immortal life that came from an immortal being so it made you immortal.
Your problem is not accident or bad roads. Why do you always think death? Even after the fall, the life of God still sustained Adam for over 900 years after God had told him he would die. The shew bread that was naturally baked, when put inside the ark lived forever because there was life in that ark and that was the life you received when you became born again. As a result of that life, the bread escaped decay. When the children of Israel ate the manna, the bible said they moved in the strength of that food for many days, because it was an immortal food. When the immortal is absent, the natural cause will take its effect.

The power of God carries an ability within it to sustain things, so it sustained that bread in the wilderness that the children of Israel ate. Their cloth and sandal didn't wear out because they were moving under God's power; an immortal ability was applied to it. All other laws were suspended because an immortal law was at work in them.
The laws of the earth are not your problem rather, the ability to take charge of the immortal life within you.
If I can't explore the immortal life within me, then I limit what God can do for me. It was this same power Moses experienced, that at 120 years his eyes were not abated. He was climbing the mountain at 120, God had to tell Moses to go and die.

Joshua 14:6.

6. "Then the children of Judah came unto Joshua in Gilgal: and Caleb the son of Jephunneh the Kenezite said unto him, Thou knowest the thing that the LORD said unto Moses the man of God concerning me and thee in Kadeshbarnea

7. Forty years old was I when Moses the servant of the LORD sent me from Kadeshbarnea to espy out the land; and I brought him word again as it was in mine heart."

Caleb was mounted upon by this same power, that at eighty five years he was fit and ready for battle. Whatever comes in contact with the life will carry the attributes of that life.
The gospel is to bring life and immortality. The life is for your spirit while the immortality is for your body because it is the body that is mortal and can be made immortal.
Life is sustained by words that come from the immortal realm.

You have the immortal life of God in you to say no to death, that's why, if anybody dies around you, you have the power to raise the person back to life.

2 Timothy 1:10.
10. "But is now made manifest by the appearing of our Saviour Jesus Christ, who hath abolished death, and hath brought life and immortality to light through the gospel."

Christ raised so many from the dead before He Himself rose from the dead and the Apostles walked in this same dimension. The immortal life is not just a possibility, it is a reality. The bible says "we should give ourselves wholly to the word until our profiting appears to all." So we keep pressing, till we come to the reality of this truth. Anything you believe, you give legal access to its manifestation in your life. If you believe you are supposed to die, then you have given legal access to death to take you but if you believe in immortality, you have given immortality a legal access to manifest in your life.
There is a power to call life into things. It is not given to certain men of God but those who have understood who they are. If you understand this, you will begin to manifest it. One thing most people are afraid of is death.

A believer should walk tall knowing he cannot die carelessly if he stays connected to God's purpose, even if you walk through the valley of the shadow of death you should fear no evil. Sometimes wrong knowledge is the problem. God has told you to choose life because no germ or disease can change it. The bible says, you have passed from death unto life (1 John 3:14).

Seek Immortality

A believer should seek immortality. Eternal life consists of Glory, honour and immortality. Jesus took the form of mortality so that He could bring many sons unto Glory before he returned to immortality to show that he existed before He came on earth. Christ had to first give up the ghost before He died. He gave up the immortal life then He died, for as long as that immortal life was in Him, death could not take a hold of him. You have that same immortal life stuck up in your spirit. Seek immortality.

Romans 2:7.
"To them who by patient continuance in well doing seek for glory and honour and immortality, eternal life."

You have power to lay down your life and to take it up. The power of death has been taken away from Satan by Jesus and given to you. The bible says all things are yours both life and death, that means you are the one who chooses the one to use per time.

So when a believer confesses death, he has already given death a legal access, that's why no matter the frustration, don't confess evil because things are changing for the better. If a believer maintains his confession, it doesn't matter how critical his state, he will be restored. It's not pride to confess that you can't die, it's your identity. The more you read the word, the more you call life to yourself. Anytime you stay in the atmosphere of worship and prayer you stir.the life of God in you. Walking in love is a way to exhibit the life of God. He that loves his brother abides in life and he that hates his brother abides in death; bitterness is one easy key to death.

CHAPTER 7
THE POWER TO BLESS (BLESSING POWER)

2 Timothy 2:15.
15. "Study to shew thyself approved unto God, a workman that needeth not to be ashamed, rightly dividing the word of truth."

The proof that you are giving yourself wholly to the word of God is that your profiting is appearing to all. If it doesn't appear to all it means knowledge is still lacking. Blessings or curses are pronouncements; wishes or written decrees with power behind it for either good or evil that will release certain activity or put in motion things that work through a generation. God has put a blessing on Abraham, such that anyone who cursed him was cursed.

Without Abraham saying a word the curse returned to the one who cursed him. In same vain, if anyone blessed him, the blessing came back to that person. The word blessing means 'empowered to prosper'. If you ever imagined evil against a child of God who is conscious of the blessing and knows who he is in Christ, you have only dug your own grave. It is a law in the spirit and Abraham didn't have much to do to work it out. You cannot fail in life because there is a blessing upon your life.

Just like you have generational curses, you have generational blessing. When you became born again, generational curses over your life died. In Christ you are called into the blessing; that consciousness kills the power of any curse.

You activate the power of the blessing by releasing words and by being conscious of the truth; when you become conscious of it and say it, you activate it. Don't worry about the economy because a blessed man is not bound by the circumstances of life.

The Blessing is Stronger than the Curse

The power of the blessing upon you makes everything work to your advantage. It doesn't matter how bad things are, it will turn out for good because for a blessed man, the power of the blessing is always at work. You cannot keep a believer down; the blessing will always take him up. Don't fix your eyes on the circumstances around you; fix your eyes on the blessing because the blessing has a way of taking you to the top.

Number 23:20.
20. "Behold, I have received commandment to bless: and he hath blessed; and I cannot reverse it."

The blessing is stronger than anything you can think of. You don't need anybody to give you money, you need someone to bless you and the bible is full of blessings. A blessed man can never be ordinary.

Genesis 27:33-38.
33. "And Isaac trembled very exceedingly, and said, Who? whereis he that hath taken venison, and brought it me, and I have eaten of all before thou camest, and have blessed him? yea, and he shall be blessed.

34. And when Esau heard the words of his father, he cried with a great and exceeding bitter cry, and said unto his father, Bless me, even me also, O my father.
35. And he said, Thy brother came with subtilty, and hath taken away thy blessing.

36. And he said, Is not he rightly named Jacob? for he hath supplanted me these two times: he took away my birthright; and, behold, now he hath taken away my blessing. And he said, Hast thou not reserved a blessing for me?

37. And Isaac answered and said unto Esau, Behold, I have made him thy lord, and all his brethren have I given to him for servants; and with corn and wine have I sustained him: and what shall I do now unto thee, my son?

38. And Esau said unto his father, Hast thou but one blessing, my father? bless me, even me also, O my father. And Esau lifted up his voice, and wept."

The blessing has the power to go backward and forward. Don't be afraid of generational curses, be conscious of generational blessing.
Your children should never suffer because you are blessed. Whatever you are going through, don't compromise because you carry a blessing that will produce millions for you. Don't sell your birthright because of hunger, it is only for a season, it is for a while. The blessing is stronger than the curse.

The blessing is stronger than what you are going through. It has a way of bringing you to honour. Jacob understood the power of the blessing and collected it from Esau. Esau gave Jacob his birthright by his words. Words are the conveyors of blessings and curses, that is why it is needful for ministers to always prophesy over the people because they are releasing the blessing.

Hebrews 7:7.
"And without all contradiction the less is blessed of the better."

 look for people that are higher than you to speak words into your life. It doesn't matter what you are going through now, the blessing is working. Joseph was in prison and the Lord was with him and made him prosperous in prison. Even though he didn't have money, the bible called him a prosperous man in prison. God looks at you by the blessing, not by your situation. Don't become a slave to a rich man because of his wealth, shake them and greet them with dignity. God has blessed you. If anybody gives you anything he's only responding to the blessing of God upon your life.
Hard work is not what makes you blessed. It's the blessing of God that makes rich and adds no sorrow. When you are blessed, you don't expect anything to get worse, you expect it to get better. There's no reversal of the blessing but you can reverse a curse, because the blessing is stronger than a curse. The bible says the path of a righteous man is as a shining light that shines brighter and brighter unto a perfect day (Proverbs 4:18). You can't go down again, you can only go up. You are moving forward. Jacob before his departure into eternity called his sons and blessed them and it happened just as he had spoken (Genesis 49).

Empowered To Bless and Be Blessed

You have been empowered to bless and to inherit a blessing.

Romans 12:14.
14. "Bless them which persecute you: bless, and curse not."

1Peter 3:9.
9. "Not rendering evil for evil, or railing for railing: but contrariwise blessing; knowing that ye are thereunto called, that ye should inherit a blessing."

A blessing is as powerful as a curse because it's the same medium you use in executing both. If anyone has power to curse, you have enough power to change it. No herbalist can curse you. A curse causeless shall not stand. Anybody who takes your name anywhere for any evil purpose, is only wasting his time. You are Lord over the master he is serving. No charm put in your office can work against you. On no account should you have a prayer request because of a herbalist, it is an unnecessary prayer request.

A curse may only work against you when you are not conscious of who you are in Christ but conscious of the curse. It's activated by the fear in you. When you are conscious of the Angels around you and who you are in Christ, nobody can curse you, not even Satan himself. When you speak the word of God, you activate the power of God. The power to bless is greater than the power to curse.

Angels and demons work by decrees. A demon works through a curse. Same also, as powerful as Angels are they work when blessings are released.
The bible says you have come into an innumerable company of angels, which means the angels that surround a believer are numerous.

Hebrews 12:22.
22. "But ye are come unto mount Sion, and unto the city of the living God, the heavenly Jerusalem, and to an INNUMERABLE company of angels."

If you know what surrounds you, you will fear nothing. When you became born again you came into a company of Angels. Round about you are myriads of angels.

These are the ones that will bring about the blessings but there has to be a pronouncement of the blessing. That is why I said a blessing is a pronouncement or a written decree concerning you. There are Angels that want to work with believers but they are handicapped because believers are not conscious of who they are in Christ and the power in them to make decrees. The bible tells us that these angels are ministering spirits.

Hebrews 1:13-14.
13. "But to which of the angels said he at any time, Sit on my right hand, until I make thine enemies thy footstool?

14. Are they not all ministering spirits, sent forth to minister for them who shall be heirs of salvation?"

The curse was destroyed when you came to Christ but the believer can resurrect it by believing more in what Satan is doing.

When a believer begins to study on the activities of demons more than the revelation of whom he is in Christ and how the Angelic operates, he begins to fail and live in fear.

CHAPTER 8
EXOUSIA POWER

This power is called "Exousia" it is a transforming power.

John 1:11-13.

11. "He came unto his own, and his own received him not.

12. But as many as received him, to them gave he POWER TO BECOME the sons of God, even to them that believe on his name:

13. Which were born, not of blood, nor of the will of the flesh, nor of the will of man, but of God."

At the point of receiving Jesus Christ you are given power to become a son of God. Sons of God are not people that are needed in heaven, they are people that have a different assignment on earth.

Exousia means "Dominion Authority". It is the ability to walk in the capacity of God's ability. It is walking in the capacity of the whole ability that exists in God. It means to walk in the capability of His ability. Exousia is a deposit of the very life of God from which we draw strength to rule. It is the impartation of the strength of heaven into a believer to function in the ability of God. It is the flow of God's ointment upon a believer to act in his ability.
Exousia Power Is Acting God
It is becoming the strength of God. That means, you are the ark of God's power. So you are the strength and defense system of heaven. Exousia doesn't just make you a messenger; it makes you the office itself. The bible says you have been given the ability to answer the cry of creation.

Romans 8:19.

19. "For the earnest expectation of the creature waiteth for the manifestation of the sons of God.

20. For the creature was made subject to vanity, not willingly, but by reason of him who hath subjected the same in hope,

21. Because the creature itself also shall be delivered from the bondage of corruption into the glorious liberty of the children of God.

22. For we know that the whole creation groaneth and travaileth in pain together until now."

Creation has been in bondage ever since the fall of Adam. The animals were not created to hurt man before Adam fell. They naturally submitted to man without being aggressive to man, because of the spiritual plane where he stood. When Adam lost his place, he handed over his dominion over earth to Satan and Satan corrupted everything that was created. All of God's creation also rebelled against man. Corruption means that something has been changed from its original form. The earth is crying for who will deliver her from the bondage of corruption.

When a man has to work like an elephant and eat like an ant it is corruption. When the bible says out of the sweat of thy brow shall thou eat, it is corruption and since then the earth has been crying to be delivered from the bondage of corruption it was brought under by the fall of Adam.

When you became born again, God gave you power to save the earth from corruption. Sons are those empowered to save the earth and snatch it back from corruption. The power given to you (Exousia) is the ability to snatch the earth from corruption.

Example of such, was when Paul set an entire city free from the influence of a girl with the spirit of divination (spirit of corruption). Another man that saved a city from corruption is a man called Elijah. Jezebel had bound the entire city with her witchcraft, she was in charge and controlled even the King. She used the King to bring corruption upon the city by making the whole city serve Baal.

Whatever doesn't answer to its maker is corrupted. Elijah, a man that stood in the presence of God, took on the four hundred prophets of Baal and broke the corruption over the people.

Exousia Power Is Territorial

Exousia power is an empowerment to take over territories. It is an ability given to you to subdue territories, principles and evil patterns by the kingdom of God. The evil in a place should stop when you come into that place because of the territorial power at work in you.

Exousia is given to you to save nations, cities and families from corruption. The power to become sons is the power to free creation from the bondage of corruption. Christ the son of God is the heir of all things and as sons, we are owners of the earth (Landlords of the earth). Exousia empowers you to use heaven's ability to renovate earth and make people's lives a reflection of heaven by heaven's principles and patterns.

It is the power given to the church to come up with such a glorious emergence that can change the world to the way things are supposed to be.

The whole world lies in wickedness but when these sons manifest, they will break the power and system of wickedness. There is always a stir when a believer mounts with this power to take over.

Galatians 4:1-2.

1. "Now I say, That the heir, as long as he is a child, differeth nothing from a servant, though he be Lord of all;

2. But is under tutors and governors until the time appointed of the father."

Sons are owners and Lords of the earth, not just spiritually but physically, because whatever is in the spirit can be established in the physical. The prophetic destiny over our lives is to manifest sonship.

The reason for Exousia is to manifest the prophetic destiny over our lives. There are two familiar words for sons and often used interchangeably in Romans 8.

Romans 8:17, 19.

17. "And if CHILDREN, then heirs; heirs of God, and joint-heirs with Christ; if so be that we suffer with him, that we may be also glorified together.

19. For the earnest expectation of the creature waiteth for the manifestation of the SONS of God."

In verse 17 the word children means "tecnon" (babes), those who have not been made perfect in Christ and their lives are still ruled by men. From verse 19 the word son means "wieos". It speaks of those who are matured and responsible to carry out heaven's mandate. Sons are the extension of God by virtue of the life of God in them.

"...Unto us a child is born, unto us a son is given." Sons are given as superiors, emperors, mighty ones and warriors. It is sons that go for battles not children.

Mighty men are people who have fought battles over and over again and have never lost any. They have given titles of 'mighty men'. Sons are mighty men who do not retreat or surrender. God gave you Exousia to confront situations, not to retreat or negotiate, you are to take over the situation. That's why God told Adam to subdue and have dominion. When you become a son, you become eligible to take up responsibilities; to take up your father's business or vision and run with it.

Exousia Is Ambassadorial Power

An ambassador is one that represents the government of his nation in another nation. It is the highest honour given to any citizen because it shows that you understand the heartbeat of the King you are representing. As an ambassador you maintain the culture and system of your kingdom in another kingdom. A man walking in Exousia is the ambassador and the embassy of God on earth. It means when people meet you, they have met with God.

2 Corinthians 5:19.
20. "Now then we are ambassadors for Christ, as though God did beseech you by us: we pray you in Christ's stead, be ye reconciled to God."

Not many of us are walking in sonship, though we claim to be sons. As sons, we are the custodians of the healing power, miracle working power, and wealth of God. You cannot walk in dunamis except you understand Exousia. Dunamis is an extension of Exousia because Exousia is what empowers you to receive dunamis.

Colossians 1:19.
19. "For it pleased the Father that in him should all fulness dwell."

Sons have equality with God. It had pleased the Father that the fullness of the Godhead should dwell bodily in Christ and of His fullness have we received.

A son is one who has received the fullness and ability of God in Him. Paul commanded God's judgment on elymas for trying to disrupt the preaching of the gospel, he expressed the anger of God on the man.

Sons are the representative of God on earth. They can change the timetable and plan of your life. Anything that was not so from the beginning is the assignment for sons to correct.

Exousia Is Sonship Power

Romans 8:17.
"And if children, then heirs; heirs of God, and joint-heirs with Christ; if so be that we suffer with him, that we may be also glorified together."

We are joint-heirs with Christ. Satan will not dread Jesus any more like he dreads us, because the same power that placed Jesus above all principalities and power is at work in us.

What made hell dread Him was what he carried inside of Him, and the same is resident in you. He said "behold I give you power to tread upon serpents and scorpions", that is the power called "Exousia". It is the power of authority. It is a power of placement.

It is the power of an office. The bible says God made Jesus the head of all principalities and that you are complete in Him (Colossians 2:10)... of that fullness have you received (John 1:16). If you understand the power of Exousia, you will not have fellowship with demons any more.

You are not in the same plain with them. You are lord over them. Exousia means to rule. It means you are a delegated authority to rule in the seat of Jesus Christ.

Psalms 110:2.
"The LORD shall send the rod of thy strength out of Zion:
rule thou in the midst of thine enemies."

You have been given power to rule 'in the midst of thine enemies'. We are not trying to conquer cosmos, we have conquered it. You are an over comer and all you need to do is exhibit your overcoming grace. Exousia power is a qualification that has nothing to do with you but all that Christ did. It takes you into all that Christ wrought, earned and gave to you as if you earned it yourself. "But as many as received him, to them gave he power to become the sons of God, even to them that believe on his name" (John 1:12). The power He gave them is Exousia: a right, a privilege, an authority. It is coming into all that belongs to someone as though it is yours.

Whatever cannot happen to Jesus Christ cannot happen to you by reason of the union you came into. Without an understanding of Exousia, you can't understand and walk in Dunamis power or any other.

CHAPTER 9
DUNAMIS POWER

Many think dunamis power is the power that raised Jesus from the dead, but that is not true. It took dunamis (Inherent power), Ischos (generated power in prayers), Exousia (power of placement) and kratos (power from the word) to come together to form what we call the power of His resurrection. The bible says "He was raised by the Glory of the Father".

Romans 6:4.
"Therefore we are buried with him by baptism into death: that like as Christ was raised up from the dead by the glory of the Father, even so we also should walk in newness of life."

Christ was raised from the dead far above principalities, powers and thrones. That means, it took thrones principalities and power to keep Jesus Christ down. He had to be raised above them because they were exerting different levels of strength.

Ephesians 1:20-21.
"Which he wrought in Christ, when he raised him from the dead, and set him at his own right hand in the heavenly places, Far above all principality, and power, and might, and dominion, and every name that is named, not only in this world, but also in that which is to come."

I now understand what the scripture meant when it said in Daniel 7:9 "that when all thrones were cast down, then the Ancients of days set His seat and sat". That scripture is actually related to Jesus Christ.

Daniel 7:9.
"I beheld till the thrones were cast down, and the Ancient of days did sit, whose garment was white as snow, and the hair of his head like the pure wool: his throne was like the fiery flame, and his wheels as burning fire."

There were all kinds of thrones but on that day, all thrones had fallen and His throne was raised with other thrones paying obeisance to this one throne. The Jews didn't kill Jesus Christ, it was principalities, powers, thrones and dominions that did.

1 Corinthians 2:8.
"Which none of the princes of this world knew: for had they known it, they would not have crucified the Lord of glory."

The bible says "if they had known they would not have crucified the Lord of Glory." So it was not the Jews that killed Him; they were only answerable to thrones, dominions and powers.
They were all playing a game according to the prince of the power of the air that walks in the sons of disobedience. Jesus said "now is the hour", so there was an hour that principalities had power over Him but a power had to be wrought in Jesus Christ to raise Him from the dead.
It was not the power that was in Jesus, it took a force to raise Him from the dead and I want us to know that death is a principality whose hand He was raised from.

The Hidden Wisdom of God

It is the wisdom of God to show unto principalities and powers mysteries that can't be explained.

1 Corinthians 2:7-8.
"But we speak the wisdom of God in a mystery, even the hidden wisdom, which God ordained before the world unto our glory: Which none of the princes of this world knew: for had they known it, they would not have crucified the Lord of glory."

It took Glory to raise Him from the dead and not power. When these four powers combine together it now becomes Glory. You can become the most dangerous person on the face of the earth if you can get the revelation of these four powers and how to apply them because hell will be too small to hold you when that happens. The principalities and powers had surveyed all the realms of power but they didn't know there was another realm of power called the Resurrection Power, that was why they thought they could kill Him.

A young man went to play football, after the game while rejoicing over the victory of his team, he said he saw a black handkerchief come and wipe his eyes and he suddenly became blind.

As a result, he went into a church where the supernatural was operational. As he stepped into the gate, he said a white handkerchief came and wiped his face and his sight was restored.

All human beings are surrounded by mysteries, whether they believe it or not, and the height you get to in life is dependent on the mystery that surrounds you. If a man is under demonic power and the servant of God does not know or cannot discern it, then he cannot help that person despite the prophecies over him. It's good you know your identity, so that you will not walk in fear and exalt the enemy.

However, it is not wise to deny the existence of certain things because of your place in Christ. Who you are in Christ only positions you to deal well with those things. The prophecies over your life are real, however, there are certain things contending with their fulfillment.

Dunamis Power Is Inherent Power

Dunamis is a kind of wisdom and yet a power. God is mysterious in the sense that the more you know Him, the more you discover that you don't know Him. The more He reveals Himself, it's like He's making it harder for you to explain Him. That's what a mystery is. You need to be taken to where death lives and where darkness has its abode before you can understand what they call dunamis power. We talked about exousia, the power of placement which defines your identity while dunamis determines your purpose; they are so close but different.

The word dunamis is not an English word, it's a Greek word and from study, what the Holy Ghost showed me, revealed that it is something that does not exist naturally. So, the best way to describe it, is to compare it to a very heavy machine that generates force.

It is also said to be like a force that is produced from a large army. The energy that is generated from Kainji dam to supply energy to the nation is large but it cannot be compared to the energy God is giving you and that energy is called Dunamis.

55

Acts 1:8.

8. "But ye shall receive power, after that the Holy Ghost is come upon you: and ye shall be witnesses unto me both in Jerusalem, and in all Judaea, and in Samaria, and unto the uttermost part of the earth."

Dunamis power is what you received when the Holy Ghost came upon you. However, this is an inherent power.

It's a resident power in your spirit. It is a potential energy. We would explore more of this when we talk about the power generated in the place of prayer (Ischos power), how dunamis power (potential energy) is transformed into Ischos power (kinetic energy).

CHAPTER 10
KRATOS POWER (POWER FROM THE WORD)

Sons are those that have a recreated Spirit through whom God can rule the world. Man loses his place when he does not have understanding, so he walks in darkness and dies like a mere man. The word of God says you are Gods, that's why He said "subdue and have dominion." It is not in the power of God to do anything. The whole world is out of course and the whole world lies in wickedness because man doesn't have an understanding of his dominion mandate.

Psalm 82:5-8.

5. "They know not, neither will they understand; they walk on in darkness: all the foundations of the earth are out of course.

6. I have said, Ye are gods; and all of you are children of the most High.

7. But ye shall die like men, and fall like one of the princes.

8. Arise, O God, judge the earth: for thou shalt inherit all nations."

God has done all He could do for man hence, he is no longer responsible for whatever is happening on the face of the earth. One of the greatest things a man can have is light (knowledge).

We are supposed to be walking with a high-tension life to bring an influence of the God life upon the face of the earth. We are supposed to administrate the grace and ability of heaven upon creation but because we know not, we die like men; we are affected by the same thing that affects the world. When somebody has the God-life in him, he is a God and not a man and he rules over things. He's an oracle and when he speaks, it becomes a law on the face of the earth.

Acts 19:20.
20. "So mightily grew the word of God and prevailed."

The word has a prevailing ability. You are born to prevail over what you are going through because you are a child of God. Be flooded with light from the word.

Be flooded with Light

One of the powers given to you to overcome is the power called "Kratos". It is the power of God's word. Once this power takes a hold of you, your words will become a territorial influence over the earth. Your lordship and dominion in life is tied to your knowledge and the light that hits your spirit per time. The bible talks about a kind of knowledge called "EPIGNOSIS" which means revealed knowledge. It is a revelation from the word that enters into the spirit of a man and makes him become a reality of what he is reading.

Ephesians 1:17-19.

17. "That the God of our Lord Jesus Christ, the Father of glory, may give unto you the spirit of wisdom and revelation in the knowledge of him:

18. The eyes of your understanding being enlightened; that ye may know what is the hope of his calling, and what the riches of the glory of his inheritance in the saints,

19. And what is the exceeding greatness of his power to us-ward who believe, according to the working of his mighty power."

The amount of light that hits your spirit determines the level of influence you command over a situation. When light hits you from the word, you will rule over what governs men.
You become a God over the limitations of the earth anytime the word of God breaks into your spirit and takes hold of you. One of the secrets of a continuous life of miracle, which is our inheritance, is the power of the word of God.

Acts 20:32.

32. "And now, brethren, I commend you to God, and to the word of his grace, which is able to build you up, and to give you an inheritance among all them which are sanctified."

The word of God is able to build you up. You must allow Gods word to be settled in your spirit and gain ascendency over your mind and over your body. The word of God must dictate to your mind, your body and environment what happens to you and not the circumstances around you. Many of us spend time building our physical bodies.
The bible says "it profits little but godly exercise profit in all things (1Timothy 4:8)". The reason for the weakness and lack of power is the absence of the word. When the enemy comes, we shiver and can't speak to things, even though we are God over him.
Light must come into your spirit, the word of God must gain ascendency. Anybody that plays with the place of the word is playing with his life.

John 1:1-3.

1. "In the beginning was the Word, and the Word was with God, and the Word was God.

2.The same was in the beginning with God.

3. All things were made by him; and without him was not any thing made that was made.

4. In him was life; and the life was the light of men.
Be Full of the Word

God is his word. So to play with the word is to take God out of your life. Jesus Christ is the word made flesh. God is a mystery but in order for Him to explain himself to man He had to become a man.

John 1:14.
14. "And the Word was made flesh, and dwelt among us, (and we beheld his glory, the glory as of the only begotten of the Father,) full of grace and truth."

God had to leave the spiritual dimension and project himself into the physical. Everything Christ did was done by the word. When He healed it was the word that healed. He sent forth his word and His word healed them (Psalm 107:20). Every time you read the word and you see Jesus, you are seeing the word made flesh.

If you take the place of the word in your life seriously you will become a testimony of Jesus Christ on the face of the earth. Before we can become the Christ, we must carry the knowledge which is the word. Until the word of God becomes Lord over your spirit, you cannot become Lord over circumstances.

The secret to acting as Lord is by getting the word of God being Lord over our spirit. When the word of God takes control of your life and heart, your life controls the situation. Jesus Christ was the walking word because he was always in the temple reading as his custom was. He allowed the word of God to enter Him and take hold of Him. He said "the words that I speak unto you are spirit and life (John 6:63)" The word of God is a living thing, it is the life of God packaged in written form.

It is the capsule of the spirit hidden within letters. It has ability to quicken whatever is dead; it has the ability to change things. Whatever God can do, His word can do because He is the word. God in spirit-form had to transform to word form and from word-form became flesh. It was in the flesh that he began to show to man the kind of testimony he could get, if he permits the word to control his life.

Sometimes your breakthrough doesn't come from your amount of prayers but in the quality and quantity of the word contained in your spirit.

This is what gives you victory in times of challenges. If you fail in life, it tells us that the strength of the word in your spirit is small. If the word is not in your spirit and you are not strong, you will fail, even if you wish to succeed. For it's not by wish, but by how much the word has taken hold of your spirit. The truth of God's word must be revealed to our Spirit, and when that truth is revealed (the epignosis), we become champions. God cannot help a man outside the agency of the word. So if God wants to make you prosperous, He plants the word of prosperity in your spirit.

That word becomes prosperity because the word becomes flesh. He told Joshua to "meditate on the word day and night and his way will be prosperous and he will have good success (Joshua 1:8)."

You can change your life by the agency of the word. A believer that does not have the word in his spirit, though he is lord, he differs not from a servant.

If Satan wants to cheat you he removes the word from your spirit and makes you believe the traditions of men. He puts fear in your spirit, thereby, making the word of God of little or none effect in your life. The word of God can be in someone, yet be unproductive because of traditions and beliefs. So you must delight in the word.

Psalms 1: 2-3.
2. "But his delight is in the law of the LORD; and in his law doth he meditate day and night.

3. And he shall be like a tree planted by the rivers of water, that bringeth forth his fruit in his season; his leaf also shall not wither; and whatsoever he doeth shall prosper."

A man, who delights in the word, enjoys constant supply of the Spirit and remains under the blessing of God. You can come to a realm where you live as though Satan doesn't exist because you understand the place of the word.

If the word doesn't grow in you, it can't prevail over the circumstance of your life. But if you carry eternity and divinity, you carry the word in your spirit and can never be defeated. The key to the victory of a believer is to know how to build himself via the word and this is what Satan wants you to ignore.

Walk in light of the Word

The word of God is God's formula for prosperity and to a life of unending exponential increase. It holds the key to causing the influence of heaven to come over every circumstance of life. You will speak to things and they will be, because the word of God is God in your life. One very important key to make the word work in your life is not just to know the word but to know how to use the word to get results.

There are Christian scholars who quote the word but live wretched lives. It's not about quoting the word but allowing the word get into your spirit. We have been under the mercy of Satan for too long, it is time for the church to take her place and ride in the high places of the earth, converting her potential power to kinetic power (the motion and moving energy of God).

The youngest believer in the world is stronger than Satan but because he lacks the power of God in him as potential energy, it becomes inactive. Fortunately, one of the ways to make the power become active is through the word. Light ignites the inherent power of God resident in you.

Effective Meditation

Luke 6:45.

"A good man out of the good treasure of his heart bringeth forth that which is good; and an evil man out of the evil treasure of his heart bringeth forth that which is evil: for of the abundance of the heart his mouth speaketh."

The key to converting the word in your spirit to becoming a visible reality is called meditation. It means to gaze your eyes on something until that thing creates a picture and becomes solidified in your mind. It is to pictorially ponder over a scripture as though you were there when Jesus was on earth. It means to go beyond mere knowledge until it becomes a reality. This is what the bible calls the Spirit of truth.

The negative form of meditation is called worry. After you have created a picture, you begin to speak from that picture, which is meditation. From the abundance of your heart the mouth speaks (Luke 6:45).

Whatever is not a reality for you become heavy for your mouth to say. When a man says he can't die, it's not boasting, he's speaking from the reality in his heart. God had to work on Abraham's mind to the point that he believed he was the father of many nations, even when he had no child.

For twenty five years Abraham did not believe. He kept taking in the word and confessing that he was the father of many nations until after 25 years of saying that, it became a picture and it was accounted to him as righteousness. The day he believed was the day God moved on his behalf.

Whatever is gotten by the word of God through meditation is sustained. Any accidental riches can accidentally fail but anything gotten by the word of God, Satan cannot bring down, because it was established by the economy of heaven.

If you want to change your status in life, change the level of the word of God that comes into you. Another word for meditation means to mutter, to converse within you. When the word hits your spirit, it becomes fire in your spirit and you can't but speak it. And when you speak it, you cause the life of God to brood over every circumstance.

2 Corinthians 3:18.

18. "But we all, with open face beholding as in a glass the glory of the Lord, are changed into the same image from glory to glory, even as by the Spirit of the Lord."

Poverty is not final you have the key to change it and that is the word. When God wants to deliver a man, He plants the word in the spirit of that man so that when he begins to meditate and mutter on that word it becomes flesh and manifests; that is how God answers prayers. Lack of God's word brings darkness and darkness signifies anything that represents lack, evil, pain, shame and sickness.

One of the tools that make meditation effective is praying in tongues. When you pray in tongues, your mind is shut from the circumstances of the world and your mind becomes unfruitful to them but fruitful to the world. It is not reading the whole word that is the key; it is the word that stands out when you read the scriptures that is the Rhema word.

Waiting on the word produces everlasting blessing. You must learn to wait on the word. Meditation can't be done in two minutes.

Learn to spend quality time with the word. The power you generate in meditation is greater than just confessing the word of God. We can spend time on facebook, on twitter, blackberry etc. If same time is invested on the word, within 6 months, your testimony will change. If you are ready to become the testimony of the word, begin to meditate on the word.

To be changed means to be metamorphosed, to change your state from poverty to wealth, from sickness to health, from the bottom to the top. Stay with the word and your profiting will appear to all regardless of the challenges and oppositions.

Though it tarries, it will come to pass. What God wants for you is to live in the consistency of the blessing, not by miracles. Miracles are sudden interventions of God on nature, but we'll keep living by miracles until the time comes when we will gain mastery in the word. Whatever you are full of is what you communicate; the words Jesus spoke were full of life. Learn to harness Kratos power.

CHAPTER 11
ISCHOS POWER

People fail and don't go far in life because they don't have power with God. Power is the ability to effect changes. Some people want to sponsor a revival, a desire or a ministry God has called them to do by their own physical energy without being sponsored by heaven. There's about to rise a glorious church: a church that will bring down Satan and the powers of darkness by destroying them with the word. You are that church! The persecution in Nigeria is happening because Satan has seen a revival coming, he has seen that a triumphant church is about to rise. Satan wants to put fear in you so that you can abandon God's project concerning your life. Paul said we are pressed on every side but we are not crushed (2 Corinthians 1:8).

Satan will throw everything to make sure it doesn't come to pass. He just wants you to give up on the prophecy over your life. He keeps bringing things, telling you it's not working, while it is working. In the midst of any challenge, stand as a Christian and begin to explore the dimensions of power you have. There is power in prayers.

Power through Prayer

The word ISCHOS which is power generated in the place of prayer is referred to as prevailing or overcoming power. It means to exert dominion; to come to a place where you dominate. It brings the testimony of what has been said about you to reality. Dunamis is powerful and it doesn't lose its strength at any time but there's need for additional strength.

Dunamis and ISCHOS are both from the Holy Ghost, but ISCHOS is an overwhelming strength that comes from the Holy Ghost and is developed from your partnership with Him in the place of prayer.
It is as though the Holy Ghost carries a realm of power that is not released until we make demand of it in the place of prayers, yet the church is missing this aspect of power contained in the Holy Ghost.

Romans 8:26.
"Likewise the Spirit also helpeth our infirmities: for we know not what we should pray for as we ought: but the Spirit itself maketh intercession for us with groanings which cannot be uttered."

The groaning is ISCHOS and it is a latent power that must be touched. Dunamis comes as a promise, it's like a gift but ISCHOS is not a gift, it is an inheritance that is contacted by the reason of labouring in the place of prayer and that is the power that will prevail in times of evil. This is not to make light of the power of dunamis but ISCHOS had to play the final perfecting role when Christ was raised from the dead.
It is the power that compels and exerts dominion over every other power and is only developed in the place of prayer.

James 5:16.
"...The effectual fervent prayer of a righteous maketh tremendous power available that is dynamic in its workings."

Men that walk in great dimension of power are men of prayer. Paul said "I pray more than ye all (1 Corinthians 14:18)". Even though he had the Holy Ghost, he had to go for a deeper energy level, that was why he could look at bar-Jesus and command him to go blind(Acts 13:11).

Prayer and Fasting

After several attempts by his disciples to perform a miracle, Jesus said to them, "this type goeth not out but by prayer and fasting" (Matthew 17:21). Fasting means to deny your flesh and engage the spirit, so you can dig deep and press into ISCHOS power.

There is no situation that cannot be changed. The challenge is that you are not ready to employ ISCHOS and take hold of God. Don't just sit down and watch things fall apart. Don't sit down and watch shame come into your life, you are a believer, you are higher and bigger than the devil, even in your sleep but you must put certain energy level to use which can be gotten in the place of prayer.

Men that cause changes are scarce because many don't want to pay the price in the place of prayer and fasting to generate prevailing power. The easiest thing to do is hear a message while the hardest thing to do is get down on your knees and pray. That's the reason for the powerlessness among believers.

The early church had a custom of prayer. The Holy Ghost has not ceased from his operations nor has the power reduced, but it is kept for those who will press in and say 'not in my shift will this evil continue, not in my time will Satan prevail again'. People celebrate the miracles of Prophet Uebert Angel, but he's a man of prayer and to prove this, he preached a message called "the physics of tongues".

The enemy is holding all that concerns you because the sleeping giant in you has refused to rise up. Satan knows he cannot dare you but because of your love for sleep, he'll rob you of so many things, and by the time you wake up, it might be too late. As such, the sleeping giant must wake up to the place of prayer. What do you think gave Elijah that confidence to dare four hundred prophets of baal? No man had dared it and Jezebel was so confident of her prophets, but a man who had learned to lockup himself in the place of prayer confronted them (1 Kings 18:25-40).Nature and situations will be at the mercy of men who will lock themselves in the place of prayer.

1 Kings 17:1.
"And Elijah the Tishbite, who was of the inhabitants of Gilead, said unto Ahab, As the Lord God of Israel liveth, before whom I stand, there shall not be dew nor rain these years, but according to my word."

The reason why you faint is because you have refused to pray. It's not that the church is powerless but the people are not willing to pray. If you don't know how to pray, your power is limited, though you carry the power of the right to be a believer and you have the Holy Ghost.

When you see that change is not effected the way you want, press in for the next energy level called ISCHOS, in the place of prayer.

Luke 18:1.
"And he spake a parable unto them to this end, that men ought always to pray, and not to faint."

God wants the church to explore the dimensions of power in him so that we can bring the whole world to a standstill and make sure the kingdom of this world truly becomes the kingdom of our God and His Christ. ISCHOS power is power with God and it is dynamic in its working. It is a power you develop when you learn to always stay with God.

This is because Satan knows it's such a destructive power that will stop him from being ruler over your life, your home and the nation, he distracts you from praying. He will allow you talk and watch the television for hours but will do anything to stop you from praying.

He knows if you can explore that depth of prayer, his time has ended in your life. Satan will give you excuses to sleep some more. He will always discourage prayer. Stop sitting down in front of the television thinking things will change. Life will never change except you change it, except by the power of a desire and that desire will ultimately lead you to prayer.

This is what causes a change. Where you are today is not God's fault, it is because you have accepted your status quo. Once you say "God I am not going to accept the status quo," things will change.

Hannah got tired of her situation and discovered things were not changing, so she prayed to the point that even Eli the priest thought she was drunk (1Samuel 1:13).

She was shifting things in the spirit and forgot about the atmosphere.Hence, caused sounds in the realm of the spirit that caused a change in her direction. Men have heard your voice for long, let heaven hear your voice too.

Esther by prayer broke the protocol of a nation, policies were shifted for her request to be granted.

She learnt to change things in the realm of the spirit and was able to save the destiny of a generation. Some of you are comfortable with a good job, marriage etc. But what God wants to give you is a territory. Even after you get the job, get married and bear children, something tells you that destiny is not yet fulfilled. Something on your inside is crying for expression.

You will never enter into their inheritance except you arise. If you learn to pray, you can change the tide of events in your family. The enemy knows that if he can make you complain and find fault in God, you will never move forward. He knows if he can make you active by coming to church but distracts you from the place of prayer he will always keep you under him.

Power with God Is Power with Men

You are called to fulfill a destiny. Satan knows there is a destiny over your life, that's why he will not watch you go like that. He will bring everything within his power to distract you. He will tell you how impossible it is, but men that learn to lock themselves in the place of prayer can change things.

If you don't learn to stand in the place of prayer, you can't stand in the place of authority physically. Men that learn to go on their knees always prevail on their legs in life. Men who learn to be in the secret place are public figures outside.

Your relevance in the secret place is your relevance outside. If you don't have authority with God in the secret, you can never have authority with men in the public.

Whatever is settled in the spirit cannot be reversed in the physical. Learn to negotiate your destiny in the realm of the spirit. The reason for our defeat is because men have not negotiated on their knees but they want to negotiate on their feet. Authority with God is authority with men. Men that learn to take hold of the day before dawn in prayers must be heard by the earth. Men cannot resist a man of prayer. Complaining will not change the atmosphere only prayer can, because, when you pray, you have power with God to prevail against men. Power to prevail among men is an endorsement and prayer is the place we get endorsed to shine in the open.

They may have tormented your family but when you arrive, a saviour emerged. Saviours are born out of Zion (Obadiah 1:21).Wake up and take charge over the destiny of your life because you cannot sit back and watch the enemy destroy it.

2 Corinthians 10:4-5.
4. "For the weapons of our warfare are not carnal, but mighty through God to the pulling down of strong holds

5. Casting down imaginations, and every high thing that exalteth itself against the knowledge of God, and bringing into captivity every thought to the obedience of Christ."

We are the display of God's strength. The reason he came was that through the church, he might show unto principalities and powers the manifold wisdom of God. So when Jesus was upon the mountain praying, He defeated Satan in the spirit that is why when He came out, His fame spread abroad.

When you deal with their father in the spirit, the demons in the physical are small. Prayer is a secret thing and a miracle is a public announcement that God has endorsed you in the secret. You can't walk in the miraculous except you know the place of prayer, except you know how to manipulate the realm of the spirit to make things work in your favour. Life doesn't give you what you deserve but what you demand in prayer we make demand of God.

Prayer power is a vehicle that will take you from where you are to the place you ought to be. It is one of the fastest vehicles in the realm of the spirit that can change the destiny of a man.

Parents should train their children on how to pray. There are Generals we celebrate today that are obviously products of thorough training in the place of prayer from a young age. Make your children understand that without prayer, they can't succeed. As air is oxygen in the physical, prayer is oxygen in the spiritual. So if you don't breathe in prayer you can't survive in the spirit. Men that learn to breathe in the spirit are giants in the spirits, and giants in the spirit are physical giants when they speak.

Prayer is Spiritual Oxygen

Prayer is the oxygen and miracle is the carbon dioxide. It's not about the noise you are making or the verses you are quoting, it's about your stature in the realm of the spirit. Demons know men of prayer.

Bishop Idahosa said when an antelope learns to take the audacity of a lion in prayer; he would scare an elephant even though it's an antelope.

When you pray, you change the chemistry of your person to the chemistry of the supernatural. If you wake up in prayer, no witch would dare you, because no fly can rest on fire. It is the lack of fire in your life that is making witches oppress you. To travail on our knees is to prevail in life.

To have authority with God is to have power with men. To overcome in the place of prayer is to overcome in the physical. You can't be denied your inheritance if you are a man of prayer. In the place of prayer you create the volume for him to fill you up, so you can manifest him.

Prayer is the vehicle that translates what is being said in the spirit into the physical. Prayer is a translator, it's a transformer.

Prophecy depends on your ability to make sure it comes to pass. So if you don't do anything, it remains that way. The change you don't desire you don't deserve. Some of you are just at the edge of your breakthrough and God is waiting for you to pray.

Angels are spurring you to birth the prophecy over your life but when you begin to sleep, you miss your time and season. There is always a season for change and that's when God starts to stir you. You begin to get uncomfortable with your state you get angry as well. That anger is not for you to hate your brother, it is to provoke the life of God in you and effect the required change. When there is no desire for a change, there is no drive for prayer and where there is no drive for prayer, there is no change at all. Arise and take a hold of God.

Taking a hold of God

Jacob wrestled with God throughout the night. Jesus Christ, though He was God, prayed throughout the night. If you must listen to your flesh then you are ready to lose your destiny. There are times your body won't feel like praying but you wait on the Spirit for energy from God and ask him for grace to pray.

Psalms 80:18.
"So will not we go back from thee: quicken us, and we will call upon thy name."

When God sees your desire to pray, He'll back you up with strength. Sometimes God gives you a burden, sometimes you must take hold of God yourself. There is need to stir yourself. If you see your friend succeeding and you are not, it is enough reason to stir yourself.

You must not be stirred up in church, if you are tired of where you are, stir up yourself. Stop waiting for a mighty message to stir you up because it may never come. Your condition should be enough to stir you to pray. When you learn to pray, you enforce the touch of God upon your situation. It takes men of prayer to challenge authority and they are oracles that nobody can handle; they are principalities and God in themselves. They are Men with prevailing strength.

This dimension of power we are talking about is what we call ISCHOS. The word ISCHOS is a Greek word that talks about a prevailing power that excels in strength. There's a dimension of strength that is about to come upon the earth through the church and it is in this strength that the flood will be ushered in. God is preparing a generation of people that will carry such a mighty strength, what the bible calls the exceeding strength. It doesn't matter what comes against us, we have so much strength to overcome it and this strength will come from an open heaven experience.

This strength enables us to make history with God so that God can make history through us. It is us partnering with heaven; and God takes advantage of that partnership to invade the earth. Legally, God does not control the earth but through our partnership.

He wants to invade the earth. God is in partnership with us not because we are strong enough but because he is strong enough and he is going to use us as the portal to exercise what he has had in mind all the while. The bible says:

John 1:50.
"Jesus answered and said unto him, Because I said unto thee, I saw thee under the fig tree, believest thou? thou shalt see greater things than these."

God wants to bring man to a reality where he is mantled by heaven and angelic activities. God is taking what belongs to Him and giving it to man so that through man, He can do terrible things in righteousness.

God is going to cause an invasion of angels that excel in strength. They are the angels that harken to the voice of His word. They come to deliver from the parliament of heaven what they planned and execute it with speed without any fear.

Open heaven is when the reality of heaven becomes one with us or when we come into a more conscious fellowship with the angels and the activities that are going on in heaven. It is when we begin to interact with the activities of heaven and use them on earth as though we were in heaven. No minister has walked in William Braham's anointing which is the Balaam's anointing.

Numbers 24:3-4.
3. "And he took up his parable, and said, Balaam the son of Beor hath said, and the man whose eyes are open hath said:

4. He hath said, which heard the words of God, which saw the vision of the Almighty, falling into a trance, but having his eyes open:"

The supernatural world and natural world were not different for him; he gained stature with God and lived continually under open heavens. Balaam had great knowledge of God to the point that he knows what altar to build in order to curse a nation. As New Testament believers, we are supposed to operate in higher levels of power. A man called Ahitophel interacted with the counsel of God so much that David had to pray to God to frustrate the counsel of Ahitophel. In ISCHOS, your union with God cause some dimensions of the reality of God to flow into your life. You don't wish it you pray it.

Strength in the Inner man

The difference between the results of when two people call the name of Jesus is largely dependent on the degree of strength in their inner man. That was why Paul prayed the prayer he prayed in Ephesians.

Ephesians 3:16.
"That he would grant you, according to the riches of his glory, to be strengthened with might by his Spirit in the inner man."

The strength you carry in your spirit determines the strength you exercise in the name when you declare it. Some time ago, certain people were faced with a situation where someone was dying. They kept declaring the name of Jesus but with little result, when I got there, I declared the name of Jesus and the person instantly was restored to life.
They were startled at what happened. It was the strength in me. The bible says "if you fail in the days of adversity how little your strength is (Proverbs 24:10)". "By strength shall no man prevail". It means you can't traffic in the spirit by your human strength.
No matter how much you wish to succeed or work hard to succeed, as long as the spiritual realm has worked against your success, you will never succeed because there is strength in the spirit that determines a man's success or failure.

You must have strength to be able to push some things and correct them in the spirit in order to succeed in life. If you don't have strength in the time of challenges, woe betides you. Some people have lost their lives, not because they were supposed to die but because there was no man of strength to stop such death. God is raising men of strength to speak with the enemy at the gate. The spiritual realm is an exponential realm, hence it is over a million times stronger than the physical realm. You are as good as dead if you are strong in the earth but not strong in the spirit. You develop spiritual strength in the place of prayer.

The Power of His Might

The word MIGHT there means ISCHOS and it is generated in the place of prayer. In these last days there's going to be clashes of government but what will make us stand and stop the evil government is the strength of God. Part of Paul's emphasis in the epistle is more on the strength of a believer. The evil ones will throw all sorts of arrows against you but what will make you prevail is that you can stand.

Ephesians 6:10, 13.
10. "Finally, my brethren, be strong in the Lord, and in the power of his might".

13. Wherefore take unto you the whole armour of God, that ye may be able to withstand in the evil day, and having done all, to stand."

Your problem is not the devil or the demon, your problem is your lack of strength because your weakness or strength is revealed when the enemy comes. Until the Holy Ghost comes upon you, you cannot be empowered. The anointing means strength which is called dunamis and dunamis is actually meant to cause change. It means to reconcile all things to the obedience of Christ. Everything must be according to the pattern of heaven.

Acts 10:38.

"How God anointed Jesus of Nazareth with the Holy Ghost and with power: who went about doing good, and healing all that were oppressed of the devil; for God was with him."

That dimension of power alone was not enough for Christ to get to the next level. Hence, he had to get another ability called ISCHOS power. At another point of his confrontation with the enemy he needed more strength. As a result, he pressed in for the prevailing power of God, the power of his might.

Philippians 2:9-10.

"Wherefore God also hath highly exalted him, and given him a name which is above every name; That at the name of Jesus every knee should bow, of things in heaven, and things in earth, and things under the earth."

The name Jesus was given to Him at birth but the bible says when He was raised from the dead, he was given another name, at that name, every knee must bow. When He was resurrected, a prevailing power took over him and he was taken to another dimension of authority. That authority could now be spread to mankind and it was so powerful that it could even be imparted. He doesn't need to be there for it to work. In the gospels, it was accounted that Jesus Christ prayed till an angel came and strengthened Him. Even though He had the Holy Ghost, He needed extra strength and it came in the place of prayer.

Luke 22:43.

"And there appeared an angel unto him from heaven, strengthening him."

If there's A Man To Pray

The reason why the gospel Paul preached prevailed was because he was a man of prayer. What did Peter say that made three thousand people turned to Christ in one day, yet these were people that killed Jesus Christ. That was the manifestation of the power of God.

Psalms 66:3.

"Say unto God, How terrible art thou in thy works! through the greatness of thy power shall thine enemies submit themselves unto thee."

Have you prayed to a level that witches will come to you, surrender and apologise without you commanding death? You have no excuse for powerlessness. God will hold us responsible for the failure of this generation, and He will hold us accountable for the evil going on in this generation, because men have not given themselves to the place of prayer to stop evil. God wants to give birth to a people of might but that might is only developed in the place of prayer.

Revelation 11:3-4.

"And I will give power unto my two witnesses, and they shall prophesy a thousand two hundred and threescore days, clothed in sackcloth. These are the two olive trees, and the two candlesticks standing before the God of the earth."

Elijah was a man that stood before God and was always standing in the midst of fire that was why, he could say "if I be a man of God, let fire come down". You can only bring down what you interact with in prayer. If you know God called you and you have a ministry, you better give yourself to prayers because sooner or later you will lose relevance before men.

Avoid all forms of distractions and insist in the place of prayer to be endued with power; power makes you relevant before men.

Revelation 11:5-6.

"And if any man will hurt them, fire proceedeth out of their mouth, and devoureth their enemies: and if any man will hurt them, he must in this manner be killed. These have power to shut heaven, that it rain not in the days of their prophecy: and have power over waters to turn them to blood, and to smite the earth with all plagues, as often as they will."

The reason they could release fire was because of where they stood. If you stand with fire, you will command fire. It is not possible for a man of God to cause change in someone else life when he interacts with the same demon and is being fed in dreams by demons.

How can he cast the demon out from an individual, when he is also in bondage? Until there's a stamp of power over you, don't go anywhere (Acts 1:4).

The Need for Men of Power

The world is not shaking because the church has no power. The bible does not leave us in doubt on where He placed Satan and where He placed us.

Nowhere in the bible was Satan given power over us, so if he has power over you it is because you have refused to take your stance in the place of prayer. If you spend time talking and spend more hours on the phone, how will you command a demon? When young people are supposed to be developing power in the place of prayer for the next generation, they spend their nights making calls to their girl friends or boyfriends.

The game of life is a game of power so why waste time on things that won't stir up and develop the power of God in you.

If you can go on six hours daily for one week you cannot but change that situation. Anytime you see a situation persisting in your home, it means it's an assignment for you to solve.

Isaiah 66 8-9.

"Who hath heard such a thing? who hath seen such things? Shall the earth be made to bring forth in one day? or shall a nation be born at once? for as soon as Zion travailed, she brought forth her children. Shall I bring to the birth, and not cause to bring forth? saith the Lord: shall I cause to bring forth, and shut the womb? saith thy God."

You can only cause change when you spend more time praying. Jesus though, He was God, knew that He needed an energy level to break evil and He went to pray. It means that deity must cultivate the habit of prayer and chanting. The reason you get provoked when evil is happening is because it doesn't fit into your assignment. If you can't transact in the spirit, you are an unproductive and a dead Christian. Jesus could not but pray because of the assignment that was before Him.

Psalms 78:9.
"The children of Ephraim, being armed and carrying bows, turned back in the day of battle."

It is not a question of being armed, it is about having strength. It's not about the armories but the strength (2 Samuel 23:8-23). The bible says "be strong in the power of His might and put on the whole amour of God", which means if you are not strong, the amour will not be useful.

Ephesians 6:9-10.
"Finally, my brethren, be strong in the Lord, and in the power of his might."

The finger of God is the strength of God.

Luke 11:20.
"But if I with the finger of God cast out devils, no doubt the kingdom of God is come upon you."

Psalms 110:2-3.
"The Lord shall send the rod of thy strength out of Zion: rule thou in the midst of thine enemies. Thy people shall be willing in the day of thy power, in the beauties of holiness from the womb of the morning: thou hast the dew of thy youth."

The rod of His strength is His power which is ISCHOS that is developed in the place of prayer.

Upgrade Your Prayer Life

Upgrade your prayer life. In the day of power the people shall be willing. Prayer makes power available.

James 5:16.
"Confess your faults one to another, and pray one for another, that ye may be healed. The effectual fervent prayer of a righteous man maketh tremendous power available that is dynamic in its workings."

The queen of England said 'I fear the prayer of John Knox more than the whole army of England' because he was a man that got things done in prayers. Your desires are fulfilled when you pray, so a prayer less person is a desire less person.
Time will tell and we'll know if you are someone who prays. I felt I was a prayer champion some years back but was proven wrong when a brother came and suggested that we pray together.

The first day we were to pray, I asked him to lead the prayer because I wanted to know how well he could pray. After he had led us in prayers for four hours stretch in tongues, he then said "now let's begin to pray." What! I thought. Let's begin to pray again after four hours? Then I knew I was a baby in the place of praying. ISCHOS means dominion and the dominion is in prayer. It is when you develop power in the place of prayer that you will break the yoke but until then you will live your life under threats from the enemy.

Genesis 27:40.
"And by thy sword shalt thou live, and shalt serve thy brother; and it shall come to pass when thou shalt have the dominion, that thou shalt break his yoke from off thy neck"

You may be born again but the demons that have contended with your Father's house and made all your uncles so useless will also prevail over you if you don't apply the necessary weapons to bring about the reality of Gods power over your life. That is not a curse, it is the truth.

Your Fathers prayed but they didn't have this knowledge but now you do . There's a reason God brought you into that family, there's a reason you were born for such a time as this. You are the change that your family needs and you know how to produce it. If you continue to sleep throughout the day and talk all night, the enemy will have an entrance because "he that breaks the edge, the serpent will bite".
You make room for the devil when you don't have a prayer life, when you don't have a bible study life and when you are among friends that don't stir you up towards the word so let go of them.

2 Kings 19:3.
"And they said unto him, Thussaith Hezekiah, This day is a day of trouble, and of rebuke, and blasphemy: for the children are come to the birth, and there is not strength to bring forth."

You may have great prophecies over your life but if you do not have strength to deliver, know now that you need strength to birth your destiny. You were not born a spectator, to watch others prosper in life while your go down the drain.
You are the owner of the earth. You have what it takes to succeed. You carry the Holy Ghost inside of you and you carry the wisdom of God, so why should you fail? Why should the heathen succeed and you fail? You need to cause a change in the spirit. You need to pray, not because you are jealous, but because you know who you are and what belongs to you. We are not competing neither are we covetous; we know our inheritance in Christ. What you need is a change, the power that will take hold of you to cause a change is in your life.
If you are called to ministry, you need power to solve problems.
You cannot watch people die of cancer and oppression and you call yourself a minister. Stop testifying about the devil.

Talk about the acts of God and not the acts of Satan. Tell yourself not on your shift will the enemy throw shame and crisis at you; not on your shift will the enemy take over your family and destiny. Produce power for change by praying in the Holy Ghost always. Some things don't answer to titles, they answer to the anointing which is developed in the place of prayer. You don't have the power to push away things or obstacles, it is the strength of God that can achieve that and that strength is invoked in the place of prayer.

The angel of strength will walk with you. See yourself prevailing in areas you have struggled before now. You must be desperate for it.

Let us explore certain men of power that walked this earth realm.

CHAPTER 12
MEN OF POWER

THE GREAT APOSTLE (BABALOLA)
The field of mysticisms and spiritual phenomena are beginning to attract the attention and loving interest of the modern age. In hunger and persistent search for reality, answers to many unanswered question of which have transcended beyond what meets the eyes and what bare hands could handle. This hunger and interest to understand spiritual things, to unearth deep mysteries of the unseen realm, and most importantly to know and intercourse with divinity has driven you to reading this book, of which I'm assured by the intensity of the spirit will not leave you frustrated. In order to understand the varied moves, manifestations and waves of God, it is essential to study the character of the founding personalities. In other words, to understand a particular fact of revival expression and phenomenon, it is essential to also visit the lives of those men and women who are genius of revival.They were men who walked in fearful dimension of Gods power.

On this basis, we'll look at the life of one of the notable figures of the Alaadura movement Joseph Ayo Babalola, a man that has been acclaimed "the central and the most notable figure in the whole Alaadura movement. Knowing that many revivals have come and gone and we talk about the exploits of those revivalists, this study is proposed to ignite a fire in us, to cause a craving in our spirit for the raw power of God and to instill a desperate hunger to carry on from where they (past revivalists) stopped to greater feats. Knowing that the later glory should be greater than the former.

Overview

Apostle Babalola: a man filled with wisdom and founder of Christ Apostolic Church (CAC). Quiet but eloquent, courageous and hardworking, the great general who possessed a super human physique, beautiful straight hair, eyes that could see further than the human eye even into the invisible, loud resounding voice, resilient body that could go for days without food or water, unusual strength, filled with the Joy of the Lord, a music lover, song writer, husband to Dorcas Adetoun, father of five, mentor to so many and father of many.

His Birth

According to parental testimony, the birth of Babalola was preceded by an unusual and unexplainable incidents; the same heavily characterized his entire life. Three months to his birth, Madam Martha Rotimi his mother contracted small pox; she was then relocated to a farm in IGBO NIYUN FOREST for treatment. One day during the dry season while Joseph's father was in his farm, something strange happened. Someone set fire on the bush leading to those (bushes) surrounding the hut where Joseph's father and mother were staying. At the sight of this, David (Joseph's father) lamented: "we are in trouble, we did not die of small pox epidemic in the town but we will now perish through this strange fire" meanwhile animals of different shapes and kind trying to escape, stopped within fifty feet radius away and began moving toward them (in the hut). While they waited for their dramatic end, without any external effort, the fire suddenly went down until it finally quenched, then the animals all went their ways the other. On the 25th of

April, 1904, the sound of a mighty thunder which was followed by a suspicious shaking accompanied the birth of Babalola to the family of Mr. / Mrs. David Rotimi of the Anglican Church in the community of ODO-OWA in IIOFA, Kwara state (Nigeria).

Seven days later, he was named Joseph Ayo Babalola. A name that distinguished him from every other member of the family as the only child who did not bear the family name; Rotimi. At his naming ceremony, it was said that bush meat was in abundance. While growing up, Joseph would say certain things and act in certain ways that were clearly above the wisdom and imagination of one at the age of 3 as he was. One day looking intently at the sky with a loving admiration, he was noticed by his mother who asked what he was looking at and he replied "can't you see what I'm seeing? I'm looking at the king of glory" this response made his mother utterly surprised. When he was seven years old, he was offered a piece of meat that had been sacrificed to an idol by his grandmother, an item which she had brought from an idolatrous ceremony. But Babalola rejected it with a resounding rebuke to her saying "mama ye Jeboyeye" meaning (grand ma, stop eating sacrifices) this resulted in her becoming a Christian. Those are some of the first signs that proved he was not an ordinary child but a carrier of God's supernatural power.

Educational and Vocational Training

At age 14, Babalola and his uncle Mr. Moses Rotimi left Odo owe for Lagos (in 1918) with educational plans in mind. He first began his education in Awori-land but on the transfer of his uncle he was enrolled at Methodist school at Ajaje at Ebute-metta in 1921 where he completed two sessions before withdrawing again in 1924. They moved to Oshogbo that same year and after a period he again enrolled at Mes School, in the town where he read up to standard five before he finally dropped out to learn trade. Within a short time he mastered blacksmithing. But had no money to buy the equipment so he began to work at a hospital to raise money. It was during this period that the public department employed him as a roller driver and paid him 4 pounds per month. At the time Babalola joined them and they were working on Akure Ijesha road, and within a short time, he had his own workforce and began to handle jobs to the satisfaction of his European supervisor, Mr. Ferguson in 1928.

His Encounter and Call

The 25th of September, 1928 was a remarkable day in Babalola's life. The day a faithless steam roller refused to work. It started about two weeks earlier. He said "I couldn't sleep for a whole week both night and day. My spirit was rejoicing and joyous as I read my bible (Psalms 1 – 150). I did not feel sleepy neither did I fall sick." Before a person can seek God, God by his sovereign grace must arrest the attention of his wandering sheep.

On the 9th of October, I was still on the roller site, at about 12noon, we heard a mighty voice that sounded like 10,000 thunders calling my name, Joseph! Joseph!! Joseph!!! Leave this work you are doing, if you don't leave this work you are doing, this year you will be cut off from the land of the living "these happened thrice but I was only concerned with getting the roller to function. Until two days later the same event repeated itself, while amidst many people including my workers. But this time the voice said "if you don't leave this work the roller would never move again. Concerned and surprised, I shouted back "who are you calling me and which work do you have for me to do?" A lot of people asked who I was speaking to after the encounter. So I finally left the job and immediately went home. The same voice again said if I wanted to know him, I should begin a seven day fast.

At mid-night on the seventh day of the fast, the Lord appeared to me physically, and asked if I wanted to eat. I replied yes. Jesus Christ stood before me in a sparkling white garment which was touching the ground but did not say anything, and there was another being that was standing reaching the sky. He gave me half a tuber of yam to eat, which I did eat, then he said, 'with that ration, I fed the world in a certain year'. The Lord gave him (Babalola) three symbolic gifts: a hand bell, an iron and a bottle of water. These three gifts as explained to Babalola were symbolic; the bell was to call people to prayer, bring the angels of God down to his meetings and drive evil forces away. The iron staff represented the apostolic authority to subdue evil forces, while the bottle of water was given to him for the healing of all sicknesses and diseases. This commission to heal was the origin of the doctrine of divine healing in Babalola's ministry and it resulted to the inception of Christ Apostolic Church. It is important to note that Babalola came to the understanding of the doctrine of divine healing by a revelation of God.

The Quest

The seven day fast had fetched him the visitation and the assignment but not the power for the assignment. Just like the Lord told his disciples to wait in Jerusalem till they be endued with power from on high, Babalola therefore continued seeking the face of God for the power of the Holy Ghost to prosecute his apostolic commission, during this time he was divinely directed to Prophet Joseph Fapohunda of whom the hand of the Lord was upon. While he waited (fasting and praying) until he received the baptism of the Holy Spirit.

A Mad Preacher

After the baptism of the Holy Spirit, he was constantly visited by angels; they brought him visions and instructions preparing him for ministry. After the angels had given Apostle Babalola a lot of revelations, they instructed him to go to Ilofa, his hometown. He gave his entire savings (14 pounds) to the fellowship leader, Prophet Joseph Fapohunda and moved to his hometown (Odo – owo). God directed him to go and warn the people of idolatry and fetish acts. God told him to go naked covering only his private part, and put ashes on his face and body. Coincidentally Babalola entered the town on a market day when the town was full of people.

They thought among themselves that he had lost his mind. He began to preach the gospel, the entire town was moved and there was great stir and consternation as people fled when they saw him, he rang the bell round the town preaching. Many people advised his father to bind him with fetters, because to them, he had gone mad. Although, the father had no understanding of his son's new act, he rejected their suggestions. He insisted his son was normal, as there was no history of madness in his ancestry.

Babalola began to prophesy to them as he preached the gospel, telling them that evil beasts would invade the town and devour the people if they do not repent. But the people rebelled against his message. And rather seized him with force and took him to the district officer at Ilorin, for him to be arrested. Despite their efforts to detain him, the district officer released

Babalola and dismissed the case. The district officer was touched by the Holy Spirit to act this way. When the people of Ilofa saw that Babalola could not be arrested in Ilorin, they sought to kill him through demonic powers, which they boasted of. They made several attempts to conjure their demonic power and charms against him but they all failed. There was a particular witch doctor, who claimed he needed just seven days but still his power failed him. As the day of the fulfillment of the prophecy of the evil beasts attack approached, they prepared resisting the beasts, to this, since they could not kill the young apostle. They sharpened their machetes and oiled their guns, getting ready to kill the beasts when they come into town.

Three days before the doom's day, the Lord told Babalola to still announce to the people that no one would be able to draw his/ her spear from its sheath or carry his/her gun when the evil beasts attack the town. The people in response to his announcement boasted of their skills and readiness for combat.

In confirmation, within fourty five days, an epidemic of small pox invaded the town. No one indeed could draw his/her sword or carry his/her gun to confront the evil beasts that infested their bodies. The word of the Lord came to pass.

At this juncture, all those who had the small pox surrendered to God by calling on the man of God and they were immediately healed. Those who were adamant and criticized him, died of the disease while others came to him for prayers and received their healing. Soon after that, a revival broke out on the Anglican Church, Babalola began to go out for early morning preaching, and open air crusades in the centre of the town. Due to persecution they were forced out of the Anglican Church. They moved to a member's house where the people received the baptism of the Holy Spirit and spoke in tongues.

Ministerial Exploits and Revival Missions

The revival missions began by bringing back to life a dead child in September, 1920. It was followed by the healing of about hundred lepers, sixty blind and fifty lame persons in three weeks. This also resulted in the desolation of churches in Illesa because their members transferred their allegiance to the revivalist; all the patients in Wesley Hospital Illesa abandoned their beds to seek healing from Babalola.

This divine kickoff of the great Revival of 1930 saw people coming from most parts of Africa and Diaspora without posters or TV adverts. In June 25th 1931, he slew the sinister Abugabu (dragon) of the jungles of yogumbo, wielding the Holy Ghost sword imbued with the fire of the Lord. Thereafter, with a bell and a Yoruba bible in his hand, he turned Yoruba land and eastern Nigeria to God, preaching repentance, renunciation of idolatry, the importance of prayer and fasting and the power of God to heal the sick. Wherever and whenever he prayed into the water for therapeutic purposes, effective healing was procured for those who drank it. Enabled by the power of the Holy Spirit; he could spend several weeks in prayer. He regularly saw angels who delivered divine messages to him. On one occasion an angel appeared in one of his prayers and forbade him to wear caps.

Babalola was invited to Illesa, so he joined the delegation of peace makers who were sent to resolve the controversy among the leaders of the faith tabernacle over doctrinal issues like the use of western and traditional drugs versus divine healing, polygamy and whether polygamous husbands should be allowed to partake of the Lord's Supper. As the reconciliatory talks were going on, suddenly a mighty sweeping revival broke out on faith tabernacle congregation at Oke-Oye, Illesa. This included raising a dead child, and healing of those afflicted with diseases. Many mighty works were performed through the use of the prayer bell and people drinking the consecrated water from a stream called Omi-Ayo (stream of Joy). As thousands were converted to the faith tabernacle, there was no space in the church hall, so revival meetings were shifted to an open field. Members claim that hopeless barren women were made fruitful, women who had been carrying their pregnancies for long years were wonderfully delivered, the dumb spoke, lunatic were cured, witches confessed and demon possessed were exorcised.

A revelation was later given to Babalola to burn down a big tree in front of the Oba's palace. The big tree was believed traditionally, to be the rendezvous of witches and wizards. The juju tree was greatly feared and sacrifices were usually made to the spirits believed to reside in it. There were apprehensions that this bold act would result to his instant death, since it was expected to arouse the anger of the gods. But amazingly, the prophet did not die, rather he grew stronger in the Lord. That single event made seven of the Oba of Illesa, the most important people in the town to fear and respect the prophet.

The wave of this revival spread from Illesa to Ibadan, Ijebu, Lagos Efon Alaaye, Aramoko, Ekiti and Abeokuta. No greater revival preceded that of Babalola. The prophet was directed by the Holy Spirit to go out on further missionary journeys accompanied by some of his disciples. He went to Offa (Kwara State), people turned out to hear his preaching and receive miracles.

The Muslims became jealous and for that reason, incited the community against him. Traditionally, the place was a forbidden forest but he established his prayer ground there and when no harm came upon them, the inhabitants were inspired to accept the new faith.

The success of the revival was accelerated by the conversion of the Oba of Efon and Oba of Aramoko in 1932, after being released from jail he was entreated to come to Calabar by Mr. Cyprian. The prophet sought God's direction and he had success. Certain members of a national church in Duke town received the gift of the Holy Spirit. When he returned and settled for a while, in 1935 he married Dorcas and the following year went to the Gold coast.

Problems and Challenges Faced by Babalola

Ayo Babalola was sent out of the Anglican church of his village by his Bishop because most members of the church saw visions, spoke in tongues and prayed vigorously. When he deduced that this behavior was caused by a swamp witch, he went into her hut where she quickly turned into a terrible bird beast. He tricked the bird-witch into eating gogundo berries from his hand allowing him to clonk her on the head and broke the curse. This led to his joining the faith Tabernacle church in November, 1929. After the revival, he retreated to his home to fortify himself spiritually.
While there, a warrant for his arrest for preaching against witches and some of their evil practices was issued and he was sentenced to six months in Benin City in March, 1932.

The spectacular evangelism brought with it a wave of persecution to all who rushed into the new faith. The mission churches became jealous and hostile. The Nigerian Faith Tabernacle was ceded to the British Apostolic Church, consequently the name changed to Apostolic Church.

Doctrinal differences began to appear, the white missionaries were found using quinine and other tablets.

The controversy could not be resolved as a result, the group split. One fraction of the church made Oko-oye its base and retained the name Apostolic Church. The other larger fraction in which Babalola was a leader became Christ Apostolic Church.
His Death

He died at age 55 on the 26th of July, 1959 as a result of illness. On the 24th he returned to Ibadan to attend the general council meeting slated for that day and on 25th, after conducting prayers for ministers and others, he sent for Bayo Adeyinka at Ede to prepare him a place to sleep. When he arrived, he requested to be allowed to have some sleep, as he had not slept for nine days due to the series of meetings.

He woke up three hours later and took some tea and slept again at 6 O'clock later on Bayo went to his room and he began to talk to him about a great convention which will soon be held at his home town, he was speaking in parable. He also sent for a prophet called Babajide and began narrating how he started ministry, then he bid everyone farewell after which, he took a nap. When he woke up he returned Bayo's covering cloth to him and he was asked why? He said "A man should sleep with his own clothes" Around 5pm, he breathed heavily three (3) times and the vibration shook the entire building before he exiled from the world. His personal attendants rushed to call Bayo Yinka and the church leaders; who started praying for his restoration. But the prayer was on, when Bayo spiritually saw that the heavenly host had come to meet the prophet and joyfully admitted him into glory.

Babalola had laid down his sword at Jesus' feet so he could not return to earth again. That same night, his corpse was arranged to be taken to Efon-Alaaya. J.A. Babalola contacted power from God through the price of consecration; of prayer and fasting, of obedience, of separation, of commitment and of self-denial.

Refrences:

1. en.wikipedia.org\wiki\joseph ayo babalola
2. www.dacb.org\..\babalola2_joseph.html

ST. JOSEPH OF CUPERTINO

St. Joseph was mystically born on 17th June, 1603. His father died before he was born. He left debts in cone works of which the creditors drove his mother, Franseca Panara from her home and she was made to give birth to her child in a stable. Joseph had an ascetic vision while at school and thus was renewed several times. Joseph was able to read but poorly. Yet infused by knowledge and supernatural light he not only surpassed ordinary men in learning of the shoes but covered some the most intricate questions.

Life and Ministry

In March 1628 Joseph became a priest at 25years of age. Due to certain limitations he had, he was often not allowed to attend choir, go to common refectory, work in procession or say mass in church. Minded and envious men even brought him before the visitation and he was sent from one lonely house of the capuchins or Francisca to another but Joseph retained his joyous spirit and submitting confidence to divine providence. He forced lots of preservation from men in the ministry. Joseph practiced mortification and Fasting to such a degree that he kept seven tents of fourty days each year and during many of those times, he tasted no food even on Thursdays and Sundays.

Ecstatic Flights and Manifestations

Joseph spent long hours alone in his room in deep meditation and was often found wandering about as if in a daze. On some occasions the friars found him in different places such as the chapel of St. Barbaua but Joseph was unaware of how he had time to go to those places. This was the Lord preparing him for special mission by giving him the gift of contcanpiation. In October 4, 1630 the town people of Cupertino held a procession in honour of St. frances of Assisi. Joseph was assisting in the procession when evidently he soared into the air and remained there immoveable because of the crowd. When he eventually came down he was so embarrassed that he fled to his mother's house to hide from the crowd. Time and experience earned him the name "the flying saint."

On one Christmas evening when Joseph heard the music of some shepherds who had come to join him in celebrating the birth of Christ, he began to dance and sing with joy and was lifted up like a bird to the high alter. He remained there for about fifteen minutes without disturbing the candles or burning his cloths. On another occasion, during the celebration in honour of St Frances, Joseph rose above the pulpit and remained there for some time with his arm outstretched and knees bent. On several occasion, Joseph would be lifted up in the air and would come down when his superiors commanded him.

His Secret

Joseph practiced the most severe forms of mortification. He scourged himself for hours, which often caused bleeding; He refused to eat bread, meat or to drink wine and lived only on fruits and herbs. This led to the deterioration of his health and often left him on the point of collapse. Joseph's life began to change considerable by the amount of spiritual exercises he engaged in. His ecstasies (Elevation) were becoming more numerous and frequent. On hearing the name of Jesus and Mary he would go into ecstasy and remain there for some time until the superior commanded him under heavy obedience to return to his senses.
He became famous for his ecstasies, and gifts of levitation. He began to attract so many pilgrims to the monastery that his superior had to transfer him from one monastery to another to avoid the commotion. Those flights were so astonishing that there was hardly any other saint is known to have received such a super-abundant gift from God.

His Trial

Joseph was greatly disturbed over this incident and wished to withdraw from public eye because he considered it a cross he must bear. Because these visions were so extraordinary, father Joseph's virtue was also tested. God himself permitted Joseph to be severely tempted by the devil. Added to this, he suffered for many years from dryness of heart,. But all these trials could not embitter his heart; he placed it within the wound of the saviour's side and preserved peace of mind. He had no other wish but to do the will of God. All of Joseph's experience brought many accusations to him. He was summoned to come for trial by the minister general in Rome.

He was sentenced to the friary at the tomb of St. Frances of Assisi (also known as the sacred comere) in Assisi. This brought great joy to him who had always dreamt of living in Assisi near the tomb of his seraphic fathers. This trial brought joy to Joseph and he concluded that this was God's plan.

He was to be tested with withdrawal of consolation, persecutions, temptations and spiritual dryness which were meant to purify his soul. Joseph experienced "dark night of his soul." HE no longer had ecstasies nor experience aridity during spiritual reading, while praying and even in celebrating mass. God seemed deaf to his pleading and he slumped into a depression far greater than he had experienced before at grottella.

The devil frequently tempted Joseph down with a great load. The devil frequently tempted Joseph in many ways which caused him to wake from night mares. These assaults lasted almost two years but Joseph, though terrorized; he was able to request from God that his soul become even firmer and stronger. God's supernatural grace had not allowed him to be tasted beyond his limits. He would often remark "it is better to consider giving up everything in this world for God's glory for it adds to our merit when we suffer for his divine majesty" To suffer for the love of God is a greater blessing and man is not worthy of it. At Assisi many people came to him for prayers and advices including the Bishop, Moon Signer Baglionimalasta.

Miracles of St. Joseph

St. Joseph lived in Assisi and spent his entire day in prayers and hours of meditations. When celebrating mass, he would often levitate. He found it difficult in breaking bread when he perceives that someone is living in serious sin. During his trial, preparation revisited the "statue of the cross" to be placed among the road leading to the grottela church. Ten men tried to place the lost cross in place but they could not lift it up. Joseph, went into ecstasy, flew up and lifted it like a piece of wood into place. At one time, he was in danger of being struck by a severe storm but through his prayers the hurricane ceased. On another occasion, through Joseph's intercession, a doctor was able to pass by without being noticed by Assassins who sought to attack and rob him on his way home to nessis. At another time the minister general of the orders was saved from drowning when he sought the intercession of St Joseph. St. Joseph told the minister general how he saw him in danger from his fall just as he was saying mass and how he prayed for his safety.

Joseph was able to appear in more than one place at the same time. On one occasion, while he was still in Assisi he was peen in the little church in Grotella, where he went into ecstasy and disappeared, another episodes recalls that an old priest, who used to be Joseph's confessor was very ill. He saw Joseph appear by the foot of his bed and reassure him that he will get well. At another time, Joseph's mother, Frances was dying and she called upon her son for help. The people present in the room noticed rays of lightening shining through the window and Frances seemed to be talking to someone, she then died whispering. "Oh Joseph my son."Joseph saw things before they happen. On one occasion, a woman asked him to pray for her two sons who were about to receive a doctorate degree, he saw that they will soon be in heaven. Few days later they died. Through visions from God, Joseph would set out for a journey he didn't know where he was going. During one of the journeys in one of the houses, A mason who had been lame for many years was healed by Joseph.

What Kept Him

St. Joseph had a burning love for God. He committed himself to much fasting and spiritual exercises which affected his health but never caused him to relent. He's often found praying at the grave of St. Frances till midnight. Joseph's sense of obedience prevailed and he said,

I look only for the will of God.
I want to obey always and look for God.
I look only for my crucified Lord.
I am happy to stay anywhere.
For everywhere I want to stay is with Holy obedience.

St. Joseph's manifestations, Esctatic flight, miracles were due to his deep fellowship and burning love for God. He didn't pray specifically for them but entered into these experiences because of long hours of fellowship with God. He commented on some occasions that he did not serve God for the sake of paradise or out of fear of hell. He further said; I long only for him and if because of my sins, should be condemned to hell, he would like to stay in a separate place from the damned because he do not want to hear them cursing God in that separate place. With all the pious of hell, he will continue to love God And he often prayed saying: "Lord I love you so much that if I know I was going to hell, I would love you the same as the greatest saint in heaven and I would say to you, send me wherever you want to."

ST.PATRICK OF IRELAND

St. Patrick was born in Rome Britain, Calpurus his father was a deacon, his grandfather Poltus a priest. Patrick was not an active because at age sixteen he was captive by a group of Irish pirates. The raids brought Patrick to Ireland where he was ensured for six years. Patrick came to believe that this was a punishment for this lack of future. He was put to herd sheep and pigs on Slenush Mountain in the country anytime. While he was a shepherd, Patrick spent much of his time praying. He often used to stay out in the forests and on the mountain and would wake up before daylight to pray in the snow, in ice coldness, in rain and he used to feel neither ill nor any slothfulness, because as he now see the spirit was burning in him at that time. St. Patrick is traditionally associated with the shamrock plant, which he used to explain the concept of trinity.

St. Patrick later escaped and returned to his family where he continued to study Christianity. He had a vision few years after returning home which made him return to Ireland to preach the gospel to the Irish. This vision prompted his study for priesthood.

His Persecutions

St. Patrick's position as a foreigner in Ireland was not an easy one. His refusal to accept gifts from kings placed him outside the normal ties of kingship, fosterage and affinity. Legally he was without protection and he was beaten and robbed of all he had put in again, perhaps awaiting execution. Patrick was also held captive for sixty days without giving details. St. Patrick converts to slavery while raiding in Ireland by Coroticus. Coroticus was described as a favour citizen of the devil and as a result of Patrick's letters to Coroticus concerning taking some of his countries into slavery, he experienced more trial. Despite all the changes he still kept on with the missionary work of God.

Miracles of St. Patrick

St. Patrick banished all snakes from Ireland- the absence of snakes in Ireland gave rise to the legend that they had all being banished by St. Patrick chasing them into the sea after they attacked him during a fourty days fast that he was undertaking on top of a hill. Evidence suggests that post-glacial Ireland natives had snakes. So far no snake has successfully migrated across the open ocean to a new terrestrial home. St. Patrick's walking stick grows into a living tree-During his evangelizing journey back to Ireland from his parent's home; he carried with him an ash wood walking stick or staff. He threw this stick into the ground wherever he was evangelizing and at the place now known as Aspatria (ash of Patrick) the message of the dogma took so long to get through to the people there that the stick had taken root by the time he was ready to move on and take a little rest.

Resurrection Miracles

St. Patrick performed a thousand miracles and many more. The blind, the lame, the deaf, the dumb, the palsied, the lunatic, the leprous, the epileptic and all who suffered any disease, did he in the name of the holy trinity restored unto the power of their limbs and unto entire health and in these good deeds he daily practiced. He rose twenty-three dead men, some whom had been many years buried, did this great revivalist revived from the dead. One day St. Patrick came to a place where two women had been buried. He ordered the earth to be removed; in the name of Christ and the people be raised up.. The two proclaimed that their idols were vain and that Christ was the true God. Many bystanders were baptized. He did not only revive these two from a double death (both temporal and eternal death) but gave spiritual resurrection to many other souls by these miracles.

St. Patrick came to a small village called Dubina. He prophesied of how great that small village would someday become. He also caused a fountain to spring up there. St. Patrick raised a prince and princess back to life after he was summoned by the king who promised that he and the whole city would be baptized into the new faith if his two children were restored. Patrick saw that as a great opportunity to gain souls, and so raised them both to life. On another occasion, a prince was once baptized but later expressed unbelief about the doctrine of resurrection and said to St. Patrick's that if he would raise his grandfather who had been buried for many days, he would believe in that resurrection which Patrick preached. Patrick signed the tomb of the grandfather with his staff, had it opened and prayed. A man of very great influence, who had been in the tomb by Patrick's signatory, came forth from the tomb. He described the torments that went on in hell while he was dead. And he was baptized. He received Christ and retired again to his sepulchers and slept in the Lord. After witnessing this miracle none doubted the truth of the resurrection.

On another occasion, a band of men who hated St. Patrick falsely accused him and his companions of stealing and sentenced them to death. Patrick raised a man from a nearby tomb and commanded his son to witness to the faith of the case which the resurrected man did. HE protested the innocence of Patrick and his companions and the deceit of the evil ones. In the presence of all, the resurrected man also showed where the alleged stolen goods-some flax where hidden, many of those who had conspired for the death of St. Patrick now became his disciples. St. Patrick was a great missionary bishop who converted a whole land from paganism, overturning the religion of the devils. He consecrated three hundred and fifty bishops, erected 700 churches and ordained 5,000 priests. In less than 30 years the greater part of Ireland was catholic. St Patrick said he is not worthy that God should bestow on him so great grace toward that nation. He baptized some many thousands of persons and many people through him were regenerated to God.

The 17th of March, popularly known as St. Patrick day is believed to be his death date and date celebrated as his feast day. The day became a feast day in the Catholic Church.

Saint Patrick's Prayer

May the strength of God pilot us, may the power of God presence fill us.
May the wisdom of God instep us.
May the hand of God protect us.
May the way of God direct us.
May the shield of God defend us.
May the host of God guard us against the snares of the evil ones, against temptation of the world.
May Christ be with us!
May Christ be before us!
Christ be over all!
May the salvation of the Lord always be ours.
This day, O Lord, and ever more; AMEN.

www.ingramcontent.com/pod-product-compliance
Lightning Source LLC
Chambersburg PA
CBHW060347050426
42449CB00011B/2863